MARK A. WERKEMA

9/27/17   G.R.

ANTIQUE MALL/ KENTWOOD

PAINT NOW, LEARN LATER

PAINT NOW, LEARN LATER

GUY R. WILLIAMS

EMERSON BOOKS, INC.
Buchanan, New York
1975

PUBLISHED 1966 BY EMERSON BOOKS, Inc.

Library of Congress Catalog Card Number: 66-19979

Second Printing, 1975

ACKNOWLEDGMENTS

The photographs in this book are reproduced by courtesy of the Trustees of the British Museum, the Trustees of the National Gallery, London, the Trustees of the Tate Gallery, London, and the Victoria and Albert Museum. The author would also like to thank Mrs. Harold S. Gilman for permission to reproduce the study of 'Mrs. Mounter at the Breakfast Table'. He is most grateful for their help.

CONTENTS

ILLUSTRATIONS

ONE

THE MATERIALS YOU WILL NEED

Between the young child who draws a portrait of its father by putting two dots and a dash in a circle and the famous artist who decorates the vaulted roof of a great cathedral with a magnificent series of frescoes there is as wide a range of abilities as can easily be imagined. You, and your talents, may fall anywhere in that enormous span. The only thing that is certain is your keenness to learn how to capture some of the interest and beauty of the world on paper or canvas, and, in doing so, to make your life richer and more exciting. We will begin, then, by listing some of the materials most readily available to the amateur artist. If you have a well-stocked paint cupboard already, you can skip the first few pages of this book. They are intended for people who are really 'just starting'.

PENCILS Pencils are everywhere. Like swarming termites that find their way into every part of a tropical landscape they turn up in pockets, pads, purses and writing cases wherever one looks. Being so popular, and ready to hand, they would seem to be ideal instruments for everyday sketching. But there are, as they say, pencils *and* pencils, and you will have to be rigorously selective if you want drawing to be a thoroughly enjoyable activity, and your work to be really expressive.

First, you will have to choose the right grade for your particular purpose.

Pencils are marketed in a good range of grades, according to the hardness or softness of their leads. Some manufacturers produce pencils as hard as 9H and as soft as 6B, but you are not likely to need a pencil anywhere near these extremes.

These are the factors you will have to take into consideration when you make your choice:

> *Hard pencils* are used by architects and draughtsmen and other people who want to make accurate drawings with fine precise lines, but they will not produce any of the black velvety tones needed to represent areas of full shadow, and so are not really as suitable for graphic work as pencils with a less limited range.

> *Soft pencils* will produce rich dark tones, but they also tend to produce smudgy, shiny and slightly oily surfaces if they are used too vigorously.

You will probably find a set of pencils consisting of an H, an HB and a B or 2B quite sufficient for your needs. Try these on a piece of good drawing paper as soon as you get them, so that you will become acquainted with the variety of tones and textures that can be produced with each. Try 'cross-hatching', or building up a dark tone with lines that run across each other at an acute angle. Try to produce an absolutely smooth gradation from light to dark by moving the side of the exposed graphite gently over the surface of the paper. You will be able to produce the widest possible variety of effects if you sharpen the pencil properly. A hard pencil can be tapered so that the point is both long and sharp, and then should be kept so. A soft pencil should be given a chisel-shaped, wedge-like point that will not lose its usefulness too quickly.

A sharp penknife can be carried safely in the pocket, but a single-sided razor blade should always be kept out of harm's way in a matchbox or similar container.

Some artists like to carry a small piece of fine glasspaper or sandpaper, for giving a pencil point its final 'touching up'.

12

CHARCOAL AND CHALKS If you want to produce some really rich dark tones in your work, and if exact draughtsmanship is not important, you can buy one of the extra thick leaded pencils sold specially for artists, available at stationery and art materials stores. Alternatively, you can draw with charcoal and chalk.

Charcoal is splendid stuff to work with. It is made commercially from vine stalks and other small branches, and it can be bought in a range of grades varying from EXTRA FINE, in which the sticks are as thin as knitting needles, to THICK, in which the sticks are as stout as strong forefingers—the latter being sometimes known as 'theatrical' charcoal. A sensitive artist can produce thin lines and thick lines with the same stick simply by altering the pressure of his hand.

The main disadvantage of charcoal is its tendency to become messy if it is not used with discretion—a hand moved carelessly across a sketch can blur the outlines most unpleasantly, for instance. To guard against such mishaps, keep a little fixative near you as you work, and spray a thin film over the surface of your drawing from time to time through one of the inexpensive atomisers sold specially for the purpose (Illustration 1). Commercially prepared fixative can be obtained from any supplier of artists' materials, but you can quite easily make your own by shredding a little white shellac into methylated spirit and then shaking the mixture until the shellac has dissolved.

To find out some of the immense resources of charcoal—resources that have made it so popular with artists for so many centuries—take a sheet of ordinary grey or brown wrapping paper and draw on it with charcoal and white chalk, using the charcoal for the shadows and chalk for the areas that are receiving full illumination (the 'lights' and 'high lights', these are often called) and leaving the paper in its original state for all the intermediate tones. A sketch that may make

13

this a little easier to understand is shown on the right of Illustration 1.

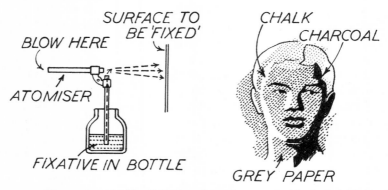

SURFACE TO BE 'FIXED'

BLOW HERE

ATOMISER

FIXATIVE IN BOTTLE

CHALK

CHARCOAL

GREY PAPER

1. Charcoal can be 'fixed' (left) and supplemented with chalk (right)

PASTELS In theory, pastels provide an excellent way of carrying colour when one is going out sketching, but in practice they have certain limitations—they smudge just as easily as charcoal, and they cannot be easily mixed to produce further shades and tints, as paints can. This means that scores of different sticks have to be bought and carried about if one wants to do work of any subtlety. Pastels do not take kindly to rough and ready forms of transport, either, as they have a marked tendency to disintegrate if they are not treated with care. However, some people like using them, so you can give them a trial if you wish.

CRAYONS Most children are given crayons almost as soon as they can hold anything at all, and these slightly waxy coloured pencils are, therefore, the first drawing materials of which the majority of people have any experience. Not many people go on using crayons after their schooldays are past, because there are so many other more pleasant materials available.

Crayoned surfaces should always be isolated with clean sheets of scrap paper to stop the colour 'travelling' and spoiling any other work placed over them.

PENS AND INK   Most artists find that they can achieve a remarkable degree of fluency with pens and ink—the fact that these are so generally used for letter-writing suggests their versatility, anyway. Rembrandt, Constantin Guys and Augustus John are outstanding examples of men who have used the swiftness and incisiveness of their pens to record the fleeting features of everyday life, adding subtlety to their drawings, in many instances, by using brushes, with diluted ink and clean water, where less positive tones were needed.

Almost any fountain pen with a strong medium or fine nib can be used for sketching, but a supply of extra ink should always be carried in case the pen runs dry.

Indian ink or 'waterproof ink' makes a fine dense alternative to ordinary fountain pen ink for drawing, but you should always use it with an ordinary penholder and nib unless you are sure that it will not clog up your fountain pen. Many Indian inks can be softened with a wash of clean water—they only become waterproof once they are actually dry.

POWDER TEMPERA COLOURS AND POSTER COLOURS   Of all the kinds of paint a beginner can choose, powder tempera colours are perhaps the most satisfactory. If they are mixed with plenty of water they can be used in thin transparent or translucent washes, like water colour. If a little water only is used, they can be built up in quite a thick 'impasto', like oil colour. These coats are quite opaque and will hide underlying colours, which is a useful property.

Powder tempera colours are prepared by several well-known colour manufacturers in an extensive range of hues, shades and tints. Many of these are marketed under alternative names, according to the manufacturer, but you should be able to obtain the following nine colours fairly easily, and you will find that they give you as good a basic 'palette' as any:

WHITE
BLACK
BROWN (Burnt Umber or Vandyke Brown)
LEMON YELLOW
CHROME YELLOW (or Gamboge)
VERMILION
CRIMSON LAKE
ULTRAMARINE BLUE
PRUSSIAN BLUE

Poster colours are not unlike powder tempera colours, but they are usually ground more finely and are sold in a moist or semi-liquid state. Spectrum or 'rainbow' colours of a quite extraordinary brilliance are included in modern poster colour ranges, and these are extremely useful when showcards, greetings cards and other examples of applied art are being carried out.

WATER COLOURS AND OIL COLOURS   Both water colours and oil colours call for a certain amount of technical skill, and so they will not be described in this chapter, but will be given fuller treatment a little later in this book. There is no point in making things more difficult for yourself, when you are learning, by choosing materials that are not immediately tractable.

PAPER   There are so many kinds of paper made nowadays that it would be misleading to prescribe any particular type. A sheet of hand made Whatman paper may be just what is required for an architectural drawing that is to be reinforced with thin washes of tone, but it would probably be much too heavy—and too expensive—for the average workaday sketch. Pads of thin bond paper are quite cheap, and are splendid for the scrawls and scribbles that an active artist wishes to make in great profusion. White cartridge paper can be bought by the block, quire or ream in a number of standard sizes and is as generally useful for all purposes as any other kind. A wise artist stores all scraps and pieces of clean paper that may come his way, whatever their quality. Brown and grey wrapping paper, tracing paper, rice paper—all these have been used at one time or another for drawings that are now regarded as cherishable works of art.

BRUSHES   Sable brushes are ideal for laying washes of thin colour or for adding mid-tones to pen-and-ink drawings, but they are comparatively delicate, and they quickly deteriorate if they are used for mixing thick stiff pigments, or for any other operation, such as cleaning a palette, that requires a stronger implement. Hoghair brushes and fitches can be used in conjunction with sable brushes and are splendid for doing the 'rough work'. All brushes will remain in good condition for a longer period of time if they are washed out thoroughly after use, and then left to dry with their hairs or bristles in a point, or a wedge, or whatever was the original shape. Never leave a brush in a pot with its hairs or bristles down, or you will probably find that it has been spoiled when you next need to use it.

OTHER MATERIALS   Among the other materials you may find useful when you are starting to draw and paint are:
   Drawing pins: These can be bought by the gross at any stationer's. Brass drawing pins are less likely to rust than the cheaper kinds.
   Erasers: Too well known to need much description. But

17

have you encountered a 'kneaded eraser', or 'putty rubber'? This can be pressed with the fingers into a fine point when a minute part of a drawing has to be erased.

Mixing palettes: These can be obtained in china ware, plastic or white enamelled metal. Household saucers can be used, of course, but specially designed palettes tend to take up less room when a lot of colours are being used.

TWO

BREAK ALL THE RULES!

Most teachers tend to have positive opinions, and some teachers tend to become quite dogmatic as they grow older—they *know* they are right! As a result of this, anyone learning to draw and paint is liable to hear various principles laid down as firmly and finally as Divine Commandments: 'IT IS WRONG TO DRAW FROM PHOTOGRAPHS' is one of these, and you will be able to think of plenty more once you have been a student for any length of time.

✴ There is only one absolutely reliable rule to remember, though, in the author's opinion, and that states that all rules in the Fine Arts are made to be broken. Don't hesitate to do exactly what you feel like doing, in other words, whenever you want to do it. It is often the experimenter, the rebel, in a class who produces the most interesting work.

USING PHOTOGRAPHS Take the use of photographs, for example. *AIRCRAFT*

In some circles, a person who uses photographs as a source of reference is regarded as some kind of cheat or charlatan, yet Walter Richard Sickert, who was one of the greatest British painters of his time, used to keep all the newspaper cuttings that he found visually stimulating, and he would 'poach' ideas from them unflinchingly. At one time, it is related, the floor of one of his studios was littered ankle-deep with newspaper photographs that were waiting to be turned to good account.

And why not? Turn over the pages of any popular journal or weekly magazine and you will probably find a score of pictures that you can enlarge, alter, add colour to or in some other

19

way improve. Choose any one of them, pin it up in front of you and see if you cannot re-create the scene represented, in your own entirely personal way, on a larger sheet of paper. Don't try to copy it slavishly, you will not get much pleasure out of a mechanical operation like that. And if you don't get much pleasure out of drawing and painting the chances are that the results will be horrible.

There are other ways in which you may find photographs and printed pictures useful, if you do not need them to stimulate your imagination. The camera is an unrivalled mechanical device for collecting and storing information. What does a lobster look like, for instance? How does a fir tree grow? What shape is the Sphinx? You may never want to include a lobster or a fir tree or the Sphinx in any of your pictures, but, on the other hand, you may. If you have a well-stocked file of cuttings, it will not take you a minute to turn up a picture of any one of them. Then, you will need to guess no longer. And guessing can be frustrating.

Of course, photographs should be used with a certain amount of discretion when you are learning to draw. The chief objection to them, as sources of reference, is their flatness. The solid forms of the world are reduced by the camera to two-dimensional representations, and these are often crude and ill-defined, especially if they have been printed on rough or absorbent paper by the cheapest possible processes of mass reproduction. Surfaces of a form that could in real life be studied and described by their subtle nuances of light and shade may, in a bad photograph, be simplified into uninspiring patches of unbroken black and white, or, as these are often crudely called, 'soot and whitewash'. If you find a photograph useful in spite of this limitation, go ahead and use it!

There is one more way in which photographs and other cuttings may be useful to you—you may enjoy actually incorporating them in the surface of your work so that they form parts of a pictorial design. Many of the most interesting and successful paintings done in the twentieth century resemble pages from a scrapbook, and would have horrified the purists who believed that pictures should be painted with carefully prepared pigments and approved vehicles and nothing else. That's another example of the way in which rules that 'worked' for one generation have to be discarded when circumstances and the climate of opinion have changed out of all recognition. So you should not hesitate to use a pair of scissors and a pot of adhesive instead of, or as well as, colours and brushes if you would enjoy doing that kind of work.

Let us take two examples of scissors and paste techniques that will give you some idea of the interesting and varied effects you can achieve.

2. A line drawing can be made more dramatic if it is converted into a black and white design

On the left of Illustration 2 you can see a figure of a workman that has been cut from an advertisement in a weekly local newspaper. On the right you can see how a really arresting

21

effect is produced if the figure is divided into two parts, one dark and one light. The outline of the lighter part is made more apparent if the background behind it is made dark, as in the illustration. A silhouette can be made by a light shape on dark or a dark shape on light with equal effectiveness.

The second example involves the repetition of a cut-out shape, with or without a certain amount of alteration. The drawing at the top of Illustration 3 shows the silhouette of a lithe hunting leopard. It was traced from a photograph in an

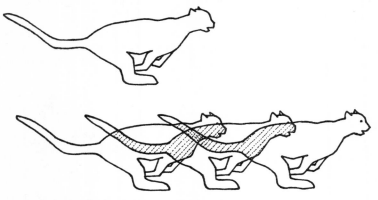

3. A simple shape can be given emphasis by repetition

old discarded periodical. The drawing below it shows how the silhouette can be cut out three times, in a translucent paper, and how the three shapes can be superimposed on each other so that an interesting design is formed, and so that a vivid impression of rapid movement is created. The leopard actually seems to be running.

A very clever commercial artist has used this device to convey the feelings aroused in a sensitive person by the scurrying crowds in London's Underground railway at rush hour. He has taken a little shape that suggests an intent traveller,

22

and he has repeated that shape, with a few subtle variations of colour, many scores of times in the small rectangular area of a single display panel. The resulting design epitomises the worried, hurrying throng that clogs up so many of London's subterranean passages each workday evening, and is a much more significant statement than any photograph or realistic representation of an Underground station would be.

So, there are two examples of unorthodox techniques used effectively, and you will certainly discover plenty more if you disregard all the rules laid down in the 'Paint as the Masters Painted' handbooks. Those rules were splendid, and had to be borne in mind when no one had ever heard of a camera, and when the artist, in his studio, was the only person who could record the outward appearance of the visible world. Nowadays, with so much recording done mechanically, you as an artist will be free to experiment in any way you like. You can distort natural appearances until they are virtually unrecognisable, if it pleases you to do so. You can abstract shapes and colours and textures from the passing show around you until nobody could identify their source, if you have an innate interest in design. You can paint standing on your head, if you feel that the results will be worth the extra effort involved in keeping your balance. All that matters is that you shall enjoy your experiments, and that after every one of them you will know a little bit more about the ever-changing panorama in front of your eyes.

Drawing and painting are, after all, only forms of research. No one with any vitality will ever be content for long with the results of other people's researches. It's up to you—if you want to enjoy your hobby to the full—to find out all you can for yourself. The next three chapters are intended to suggest a few of the ways in which you can start.

THREE

Shut your eyes and run your fingers over a piece of fur. Then, without opening your eyes, touch a brick wall, a knitted garment and a sheet of glass. The sensation at your finger-tips will be entirely different in each case. That is because the surface textures of all four materials are so entirely different.

Textures, then, are important. It will be just as necessary for you to be conscious of them when you have your eyes open as when you are feeling your way round in the dark. But most people who are starting to draw and paint cease to be aware of textures once they start studying light and shade, and colour, and other qualities with immediate appeal to the eyes. So, try a few simple experiments, using some of the surface textures you can produce with objects that are easily found. You may enjoy the opportunities these give you for improvisation and spontaneous discovery.

THUMB PRINTS AND FINGER PRINTS You will almost certainly have noticed how keen detectives are on collecting finger prints, and with very good reason. You can use your own finger ends and thumbs to produce some very interesting textures. This is how it is done:

Take a sheet of white paper of any reasonable size, and some poster colour, powder tempera colour or linoleum block ink. Roll or smear the paint or ink out on a tile or flat slab, charge the under surface of the end of your thumb or forefinger with colour, and dab it on to the paper in as many different ways as you can think of. Make a straight row of prints that are practically touching each other, for instance. Then make a row arranged in a one-up, one-down fashion beneath it. Then

24

make a straight row, and carry on like this alternately, as shown in Illustration 4. Try moving your hand in a series of circles and semi-circles as you print. Try making a number of prints with a partially charged finger or thumb. Then, if you don't mind getting a bit messy, try painting a small picture using your fingers alone—and no brushes. You may not want to keep the 'composition' that results, but you will have learned to tackle your work in a free, uninhibited way, and this is a lesson that may prove extremely valuable.

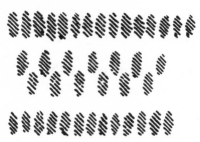

4. Thumb prints and finger prints can be used for decorative purposes in many different ways

PRINTING WITH LEAVES Have you ever picked up and studied a skeleton leaf—one from which all the soft green fleshy matter has rotted away? If you have, you will have noticed the delicate, lace-like quality of the remaining tracery. This can be reproduced quite easily if you roll out a little linoleum block ink on a sheet of thick glass or a flat tile and then apply an even coat of the ink to one side of the skeleton. If, then, you place the leaf inked side down on a clean sheet of paper, cover it with two or more sheets (clean scrap will do) and apply some firm pressure you will transfer the ink from the tracery to the paper.

Many fresh leaves, ferns and flat stones can be used for producing interesting textures in exactly the same way. The

25

grain of a piece of wood can be reproduced, too, and can look extremely attractive.

As a further experiment in this direction take a small piece of widely meshed curtain netting, pin it over a piece of clean paper on a drawing board and run an inked roller carefully across it. The mesh will then be reproduced 'in negative' on the paper when the actual material has been removed.

STICK PRINTING   When you have exhausted the possibilities of printing with your fingers and thumbs, look around for some cylindrical pieces of wood ('dowelling', this is usually called) or some that are square in section, like those in the first drawing in Illustration 5. The ends of these pieces can then be shaped with a sharp knife so that each forms a single unit for a repeat pattern. Don't cut *towards* yourself, incidentally, in case the knife slips.

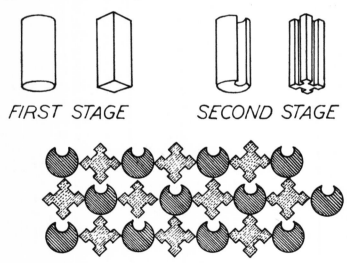

FIRST STAGE   SECOND STAGE

5. Stick printing is a really enjoyable activity for long winter evenings

You can use poster colours or powder tempera colours reinforced with a little paste for printing with sticks. If you are going to use water colours add a little white to the pigments to give them 'body'. Make a small charging pad by putting a piece of felt or some other soft thick fabric in a saucer or tin lid, and feed sufficient colour into this for you to be able to charge the ends of your sticks between each impression.

Not all papers are suitable for stick printing. To take the colours easily, a paper should have a slightly absorbent surface. If you are in doubt, put one corner of the paper on the tip of your tongue. If it is sufficiently absorbent, the part you have touched with your tongue should be slightly darker than the rest. All papers will respond to simple printing methods more satisfactorily if a pad made from several sheets of soft paper or cloth is placed beneath them.

With three or four sticks you will be able to produce a surprising variety of patterns and textures. The example shown at the bottom of Illustration 5 will probably show you how necessary it will be for you to draw guide lines lightly on the paper before you start to print a closely integrated pattern over a large surface. This example, being reproduced in black and white, can give only a very rough idea of the richness of a similar design carried out in two or more colours.

POTATO PRINTING   The humble potato is also extremely useful for making patterns and textures.

Take a potato that is about the size of a hen's egg. Slice it in half, as shown in Illustration 6, and charge the roughly circular cut end with colour. Press this on a piece of paper, and you should get a roughly circular imprint. If you don't, you probably have not made a perfectly flat printing surface, so you will have to slice again. Alternatively, you may not have put a sufficiently thick pressure pad under the paper on which you are printing.

When you are satisfied, cut the potato block in any way you think may produce an interesting texture or pattern. You can trim it so that it makes a series of square or oblong imprints, for example, varying their intensity by making several prints before you re-charge the block. This is shown at (b) in Illustration 6. You can cut chips from, and channels in, the printing surface, as shown at (c). You can vary a pattern by printing with the block held in several different ways, as at (d). You can produce a rich chessboard effect by printing with two different blocks alternately, each block having its own colour, as at (e). You will be able to invent many more ways of producing interesting textures and patterns with a potato if you do a little experimenting. In fact, as an occupation for a wet day or a long winter evening potato printing is hard to beat.

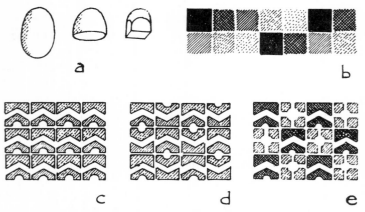

6. Some rich and varied patterns can be produced
with a humble potato

LINOLEUM BLOCK PRINTING   A piece of potato has a very limited life—it is difficult to print from a potato block for long, however much you like it, without a certain amount of dete-

28

rioration setting in, and it is virtually impossible to store a cut potato without some form of distortion happening. A more permanent printing block can be made from a piece of linoleum —ordinary household lino will do, as long as it has not been glazed or varnished. The 'waste' areas can be cut away with knives or gouges, or with the special cutters sold at most artists' materials shops. Once you have done the cutting, glue the lino to a flat piece of wood, to make printing easier.

As any lino blocks you use may well have a larger surface than the sticks and potato blocks just described, the problem of applying sufficient pressure to make satisfactory imprints may present a little difficulty. There are several possible solutions—you can attach a handle to the wooden backing so that you can take a firmer grip; you can strike the back of the block gently with a hammer or a mallet; you can use a handpress or a copying press if you have one; or you can rub the paper carefully down on to the inked block with a bone folder or the back of a spoon. An extra sheet or two of paper placed on top of the paper actually receiving the ink will minimise the risk of tearing.

RUBBINGS Put a piece of thin strong paper over a penny and rub it with the point of the softest pencil you have. As you rub, an image of the underlying design will appear on the paper, and if you keep the paper still the reproduction will be remarkably accurate. You can make a most interesting collection of rubbings by substituting other surfaces for that of the coin. Pasted on a single mount, a dozen different examples will make a very informative display, and they may provide you with some raw material for your paintings when you are short of ideas.

A great many noblemen and other worthy people of the Middle Ages are represented in memorial brasses mounted in the walls and floors of churches abroad. These plates record the physical appearance of the men they commemorate, and some-times that of their wives, children and even their dogs in a graphic and decorative way, often with a most artistic treat-ment of drapery, hair, ruffles and other details. You can take rubbings from memorial brasses in exactly the same way as you can take rubbings from coins, but as their area is so very much greater you will find it rather a laborious process if you use a pencil. Instead, use a lump of cobblers' wax or heel-ball, which will leave a dense black patina on the paper where the underlying plate is not incised.

Brass rubbings are often decorative enough to be used as wall hangings most satisfactorily. If you want to heighten your appreciation of good design—and that, after all, is very im-portant when you are learning to draw and paint—you should surround yourself with examples of the works of as many fine designers as possible.

Most of the men who made the memorial brasses were certainly that.

STENCILS   When you hear the word 'stencil' you may well think of the crude designs pierced in waxed paper, the hard intractable cakes of colour, and the cheap stub brushes that are put together in cardboard boxes and sold as sets to be given to children. Stencils can be used to produce some very rich and attractive repeating patterns, though, each of which may contain a good variety of textures. You will only need a small piece of card, a sheet of paper, some water colour, poster colour or powder tempera colour and a small block of sponge rubber, and you will be fully equipped.

First, you should take the card and fold it in two, as in the first drawing in Illustration 7. Then you should cut it or tear it so that it will form, when you open it out, an interesting shape, as in the second and third drawings. The profile of this template can then be used as an 'edge stencil', and it will produce the pattern shown in the lower part of the illustration. Sponge rubber is a splendid material for stencilling—it will produce a most subtly graded tone even in the hands of a relatively unskilled operator. And, being so absorbent, it will not need re-charging nearly as often as one of the short-haired stencil brushes so often recommended.

If you want to stencil patterns on to fabrics, use some of the colours sold specially for this purpose under proprietary names

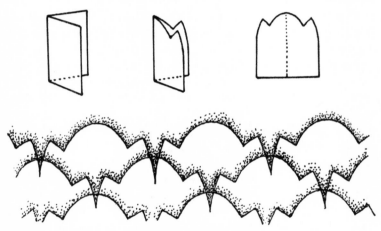

7. A piece of card can be cut and used as an 'edge stencil'

—ask your local art materials dealer for information about them. They can be thinned with distilled turpentine or with some of the specially prepared stencilling medium also marketed. If you want to stencil patterns on to wood, china, glass, metal or any other smooth hard material you can use ordinary oil colours, diluting them when necessary with stencilling medium. Oil colours used in this way can be safely washed when they are dry as long as lukewarm water is used, with a little pure soap.

CANDLE WAXES Take an old piece of candlestick and sharpen one end so that it resembles a blunt crayon—so that you can draw with it, in fact.

Then take a piece of drawing paper and make a design on it with the candle end. Any design will do, for your first experiments with this particular technique. You can plan more deliberately when you have had a chance to study the characteristic effects of the incompatibility of wax and water-bound colours.

Then mix up some water colour or a thin solution of powder tempera colour and wash it over the design with a large sable brush. The colour will shrink away from all the parts of the paper that have been treated with wax, and it will react quite normally to the unwaxed surfaces. In places, it may collect in a haphazard conglomeration of globules and droplets that make, by their very lack of cohesion, a most interesting and attractive texture.

Once you are used to this wax-and-water technique, you will be able to think without much difficulty of various ways of using it. Try drawing some birds and animals and fishes with a candle, for instance, on a single sheet of paper. Then try to pick out each with a wash of a suitable colour, each motif having its own hue or shade or tint. The resulting design could well give you ideas for a most arresting poster for your next party or sports function.

ENGRAVED TEXTURES Find, if you can, a piece of wood that is about the size of your hand and as nearly perfectly flat as possible. Then take a safety pin or some similar sharp pointed implement and make a number of curved scratches in one of the larger surfaces, very much as if you are making a scribbled texture with a pencil or pen. Then brush some ink or dark paint over the scratched surface so that the engraved lines collect a certain amount of the colouring matter. Then wipe the surrounding areas as clean as possible with a piece of scrap rag, and you will be left with a most interesting texture. Once you have created, and examined, one engraved texture of this kind you may feel like inventing a few more. Try contrasting a series of engraved criss-cross lines with a number of pin pricks or larger indentations, for example. It is a technique that has been used intermittently since classical times.

COLLAGES Have you ever seen one of the extremely decorative pictures made in Victorian times by zealous children who sewed various patches of coloured materials to a canvas background and then embellished them with silks, pearl buttons, sequins and other small accessories from the family workbasket? If you have, you will understand the enthusiasm with which certain modern painters assemble pieces of wallpaper, netting, muslins and gauzes, wire, gear wheels and other *objets trouvées*, fasten them to base boards, surround them with luxurious frames, and sell them for quite enviable prices. While it is not suggested that you will ever become immensely wealthy by mounting 'collages', as these scrap-book pictures are often called, it is certain that you can get a lot of pleasure and amusement from spending a few hours occasionally in non-representational designing with wallpapers, cloths, foils, laces and other discarded materials you can pick up at home. You will be developing an appreciation of shape, colour, pattern and balance as you work, too, as well as a feeling for texture.

WHY EXPERIMENT? If you have been taught to think of drawing and painting primarily as ways of representing natural appearances, you may wonder how the processes described in this chapter can possibly help you to develop as an artist.

You will appreciate the usefulness of unorthodox techniques if you consider the development of a great artist like Georges

Rouault. Rouault, whose paintings are known and admired all over the world, came from a family of workers in stained glass. From his earliest years, he was used to seeing the vibrant colours of transparent and translucent glass shapes around him, each framed with black, opaque bands of lead mounting. Inevitably, he learned to translate the glowing, spectacular patterns they made into terms of ink and pigment. At first, his paintings shocked many of the connoisseurs who were collecting more conventional works, but it was not long before the magnificently lustrous designs he created were accepted as some of the finest examples of the contemporary form of expression.

FOUR

I WANT TO PAINT A SUNSET!

'What a beautiful sunset! I wonder if I can make a painting of it?'

That is a remark frequently heard where people are learning to paint. The ambition is laudable, but the results are usually disastrous. No beginner ever seems to be able to catch the almost theatrical effects of an evening sky, and few accomplished artists are rash enough to attempt such a hazardous enterprise.

Why is this so? If we understand the difficulties of naturalistic painting we are well on the way to overcoming them.

Let us consider light, first, and shade, which is the result of the absence of light.

Without light, we would have to find our way round the world by our sense of touch, or by some other sense that we might develop to take the place of sight. Fortunately, we each have some fantastically intricate and sensitive arrangements of nerves and membranes in our heads that receive innumerable visual messages simultaneously and translate them into the information we need with the accuracy and speed of computers. A certain number of these messages tell us about the colours in front of us; others register the 'tone' or relative amount of light and dark in each part of the scene. A painting of a sunset—or of anything else—that does not satisfy us may well be a failure because the messages received by the artist have been misunderstood.

Let's see how this can happen in the case of a sunset.

The lightest feature in a sunlit landscape will obviously be the sun, since this is the source of all natural light.

But most beginners will say to themselves 'The setting sun is red!' and they will put a circular patch of bright pure red somewhere near the centre of their picture.

Now red, as it comes from the colour box, is considerably darker than white paper or white paint—in fact, it may be equivalent in tone value to a rich green or a mid grey. In order to be accurate tonally, everything else in that picture must be even darker than that. But how many people, when they are learning to paint, will be perceptive enough to use medium and dark tones exclusively to represent a sunlit sky? Once a tone lighter than the 'sun' creeps in, an element of untruth and distortion will creep in with it. That's why it will be so important for you to study relative tone values if you want your paintings to be convincingly representational.

As the first exercise in the use of tones (as opposed to lines, colours or textures) take a pen full of ink and flick it towards a sheet of clean paper so that a number of blots and spatches are formed, in an entirely haphazard way. Then gaze for a few minutes at the accidental pattern you have formed and see if the dark and light shapes do not suggest some kind of a picture—a view in a crowded market, for instance, or a group of boats bathed by strong sunlight on a beach. As soon as you have seen some kind of an image take a pen or brush and scribble freely over the spaces between the blots so that the picture becomes more complete. You will probably find, when you have finished, that the dark patches have been converted into cast shadows. They will represent the areas of ground on which no sunlight falls, the black, dramatic profiles thrown by the solid forms in your composition.

Next, you will find it helpful to carry out a little drawing or painting using the shadows alone.

For this, you should collect two or three dolls, model animals or other simple forms, and you should put them on a sheet of white paper under a single strong light—an ordinary electric light bulb shaded so that it resembles a spotlight will do splendidly. Then take a stick of charcoal, a very soft pencil, or a brushful of Indian ink or black water colour, and try to reproduce, on the paper, as exactly as you can the silhouettes of the cast shadows as you see them when looking from any one fixed viewpoint. While you are doing this you will almost certainly learn one very valuable lesson: you will find that the shapes of the shadows will become more apparent, and therefore easier to reproduce, if you look at them through half-closed or nearly closed eyes. This way of viewing the world reduces the impact of glare, bright colours and other distracting influences, and simplifies the tonal pattern before the spectator into a few well-defined shapes. Some artists seem to spend a lot of their lives peering outwards through the narrow slits between apparently blinding eyelids.

In trying such an exercise, you may find it difficult to build up a consistently dark tone with a pencil, even a very soft one. A bit of practice is essential, as it is when one is trying to acquire so many human skills.

So, take a piece of clean paper, draw a number of squares on it, each of which is, say, 1 in. × 1 in., and try to make them black, with a pencil, in quite different ways—first, by moving the 'lead' horizontally across the paper; then vertically; then diagonally; and, finally, by superimposing faint layers of tone, each made by moving the pencil in a different direction. If you do this carefully, you should manage to cover this last square with a dark tone of remarkable evenness and intensity, free from the nasty shine that results from hasty scribbling.

A drawing that is intended to reproduce a number of forms by recording the light that falls on them, their shaded surfaces and the shadows they throw need not necessarily employ the fullest possible range of tones between white and black. Often, a picture that is restricted to a limited tone range will be just as effective as a picture in which all the stops have been pulled out, tonally speaking. In Illustration 8 you can see how four everyday objects—a cup, a saucer, a teaspoon and a book— could be sketched in an uninhibited, bang-down-the-blacks way (left) and with a little more subtlety (right). The colours used, if this were a painting, would obviously be affected by the range of tones or 'key'.

8. Two ways of using tone to represent 'light and shade'

5 [BASIC FORMS] Once you have made yourself aware of the constantly changing patterns of dark and light in front of your eyes, you will be able to study the variations of tone on the surfaces of a number of household objects, each of which will incorporate one or more basic forms. If you are wondering what the forms are that artists refer to as 'basic', look at Illustration 9 where the five most fundamental solid shapes are shown pictorially. A perceptive artist tries to analyse into their constituent parts the bewildering forms he sees in the world around him, simplifying them in the process, as the shark shown in the drawing on the left of Illustration 10 has been simplified in the drawing on the right of that illustration.

Shading, then, becomes relatively straightforward—it need not necessarily be just a matter of copying semi-photographic-

CUBE   SPHERE CYLINDER CONE   PYRAMID

9. All artists who try to represent the natural world are constantly aware of these simple forms

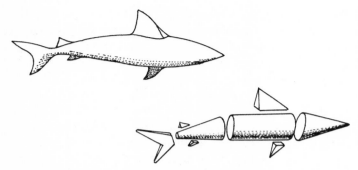

10. This shows how subtle natural forms can be resolved into forms that are a little easier to understand

ally the tones that result from an accidental set of lighting conditions. Let us take one or two examples.

First, let us consider the difference between a form that would be, if simplified, a cube, and a form that would be, if simplified, a cylinder.

Illustration 11 shows a cardboard carton and a stone jar. On the right of each, there is a shaded sketch that will give

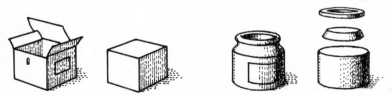

11. Everyday objects, too, can be resolved into simple forms, to make accurate drawing a little easier

you some idea of how the carton and the jar might appear if all the embellishments were removed, and the roughnesses smoothed out. In all four drawings, the form illustrated is lit strongly from the left side. You will notice at once the difference between the two distributions of light and dark. There is a sharp contrast between the tones on the various flat surfaces

39

of the cube, but the curved surfaces of the cylinder produce tones that merge into one another almost imperceptibly. This beautiful effect is known to artists as 'gradation,' and is often used to suggest the subtle changes of plane in gently rounded forms, such as those found in the face and other visible parts of the body.

The surface of the cylinder is not at its lightest on the extreme left hand side, you will notice. There is a narrow band of tone beyond it, made by the surfaces that are not deflecting light directly towards the eye. Similarly, there is a comparatively light band, caused by the oblique reflection of light rays from behind the cylinder, on the extreme right hand side, between the darkest area and the outside boundary of the form. If you fail to observe these subtle nuances of tone you will never succeed in building up really convincing representations of cylindrical forms—or of any other forms, for that matter.

Once you have learned how to use tone to differentiate between flat and curved surfaces, you will find it quite easy to differentiate between cones and pyramids, and to represent spherical forms. Illustration 9 shows how each of these would appear under a side light, and Illustration 12 shows a rather larger sphere with (right) a view of a nearly spherical teapot for which this sketch acted as a guide. You will notice that a shadow has been thrown on the surface that supports the teapot. Cast shadows, then, are the next factor to consider.

CAST SHADOWS You should always notice the shape and intensity of cast shadows, even if you do not intend to repro-

12. A teapot may be only a sphere in disguise

duce them in any particular drawing or painting. For one thing, they are so informative. The cast shadow under the teapot in Illustration 12 tells us that the pot is actually standing on a flat surface. If it were suspended above that surface there would probably be a perceptible gap between the shadowed side of the pot and the shadow on the surface, as shown in Illustration 13. Notice, in this illustration, how the shape of the shadow is affected by the raised side of the tray. Such alterations in the profile of a shadow can tell an artist a lot about changes of plane that would otherwise be almost imperceptible.

13. The cast shadow tells us that the teapot is not standing on the tray

SO YOU WANT TO PAINT A SUNSET! By now, if you have read this chapter attentively, you will have gleaned enough information to be able to have a shot, at least, at drawing or painting a picture of a landscape in which the sun is visible in the sky. If you succeed in doing this convincingly you will find all your subsequent studies of 'chiaroscuro'—which is the Italianate word used by many artists to describe light and shade—comparatively easy.

First, draw a circle that represents the sun above a line that represents the horizon, as shown at (a) in Illustration 14.

Then shade or tint the sky lightly, so that the sun, left white, seems slightly luminous by contrast with it, as in Illustration 14(b).

Then add any trees, figures, buildings, boats or other ingredients you may need for completing the picture, adding dark tones to each of the surfaces that are turned away from the sun, and leaving (or restoring) whiteness wherever a surface faces the light. This is shown in Illustration 14 (c).

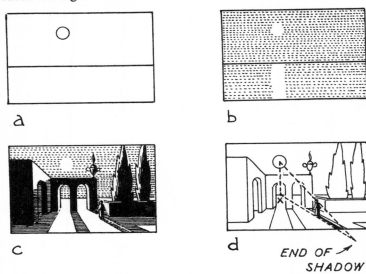

END OF SHADOW

14. The light and shade of a picture can be most easily built up in easy stages, like this

Finally, indicate the shape and position of the cast shadows. You will understand how each is constructed if you examine the dotted lines on the right hand side of Illustration 14 (d). These show how the shadow of the little man on the near side of the central arches is plotted. First, a point 'X' is found on the horizon, immediately beneath the sun. Lines that radiate from this point determine the direction of the cast shadows. Lines drawn from the sun to the highest point of each object, and then produced, determine their length.

As you sketch in the last cast shadow you should find that your picture has acquired real depth and vitality.

Most people are fascinated by the sight of a rainbow in the sky—even a young child will stop a game to gaze up entranced at one of the brightly coloured arcs that appear and then fade again so tantalisingly in showery weather. If you understand how a rainbow is formed, and if you can remember the colours of which it is constituted in their right order, you will be well on the way to knowing as much of the theory of colour as any spare-time painter needs to know.

Illustration 15 shows what happens when a ray of 'white' light is passed through a prism, or piece of glass that resembles an equilateral triangle in section. Each of the colours of which the white light is composed is 'refracted' or bent at a different angle, according to its wave length. If a plain screen (or sheet of paper) is placed in such a position that it intercepts the rays of light a miniature rainbow (or section of one) will appear. The colours, as they are usually labelled, are:

RED, ORANGE, YELLOW, GREEN, BLUE, INDIGO, VIOLET in that order. Actually, each colour merges into the next without any sharply defined dividing line. The first few bands could, therefore, be rendered like this:

RED, RED-ORANGE, ORANGE, ORANGE-YELLOW, YELLOW... and so on. But for most purposes it is sufficient to sub-divide the spectrum very simply.

EARTH COLOURS   The colours of the spectrum can be reproduced in terms of paint by modern chemical methods with a fair degree of accuracy and a fair degree of permanence. In the dull days before the laboratory came to the aid of the studio, most of an artist's basic pigments were made from

43

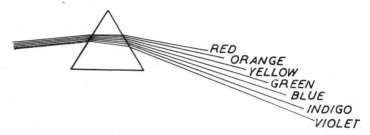

15. This shows how 'white' light can be divided, as it passes through a prism, into the colours of the rainbow or spectrum

ground-up earths, minerals and similar materials. Some earth colours are still in use today, and very valuable they are, too. Raw and burnt umber, raw and burnt sienna, yellow ochre, light red—all these are comparatively cheap, and will produce, in mixture or in combination with other colours, some very delightful colour harmonies. Their chief disadvantage is, of course, their lack of brilliance. If you want to make a painting of a rainbow or of any other really bright spectacle you will have to leave your earth colours aside and use what is usually known as a 'spectrum palette' instead.

MIXING COLOURS   One of the most delightful surprises one can ever experience is the discovery we make when we start to play with the colours in our very first paintbox. Even a number of hues as small as four will produce an almost infinite range of shades and tints when combined together in different proportions, or with black or white, or both. It may help you, when you are mixing colours for painting, to study some of the physical properties of light. On the other hand, you may find some of the theoretical knowledge at your disposal confusing and, therefore, stultifying. It all depends on the kind of person you are. Use colour intuitively, if that is the way that seems to suit you.

If you would like to do a little research into the possibilities of colour mixing—and, incidentally, to improve your own technical accomplishments in the process—draw nine 1 in. squares on a piece of clean white paper, as shown at (a) in Illustration 16. Paint the left hand square white (or leave it white, if you are using water colour). Then paint the right hand square with as intense a black as you have at your disposal. Then paint the middle square bright red—vermilion or scarlet lake would be quite satisfactory—as at (b). Then see if you can mix just the right amounts of white (or water) with the red to produce the intermediate tints to the left of the pure colour and the right amounts of black with the red to produce the intermediate shades to the right. When you have finished, you should have a band that becomes darker in tone by exactly the same amount between each pair of squares. Look at illustration 16 (c) and you should understand what is meant by this.

Next, you should try the same procedure with blue, and with yellow. In neither case should the hue (or pure colour) be placed in the middle of the strip. The yellow should be placed in the third or fourth square from the left—quite near the white, in other words. The blue should be placed in the third or fourth square from the right, which will be quite near the black. The reason for this will be obvious if you look at Illustration 16 (d) and (e). Fewer steps are needed to move from white to yellow than from yellow to black. Fewer steps are needed to move from blue to black than from white to blue. Each pure spectrum colour has its own particular tone value—if you are made aware of that, by these simple exercises, they will have fulfilled a useful purpose.

As a further guide to the possibilities of colour mixing take some of the intermediate shades of red, yellow and blue and add varying amounts of white to them. Then take some of the intermediate tints and add varying amounts of black to them. You will produce some lovely subtle mixtures by these methods.

45

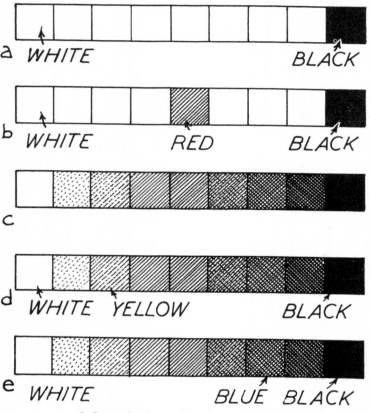

a WHITE   BLACK

b WHITE   RED   BLACK

c

d WHITE YELLOW   BLACK

e WHITE   BLUE BLACK

16. Some simple exercises in colour mixing

When you have investigated the resources of (say) white, yellow and black thoroughly, set yourself the task of painting a picture with these three colours alone. Choose some exciting subject such as a storm at sea, a whale hunt or a fight between two knights in armour and let your brush move as swiftly and decisively as you dare, both to mix the colours and to apply them to the paper. You will probably be surprised by the apparently colourful effects you can produce with such a limited palette—your picture may well be much more sonorous and attractive than a picture painted with the full gamut of a well-stocked colour-box. Look at the pictures painted by Picasso in his early 'Blue Period' if you want to see the powerful results of well-planned economy, in the hands of a Master.

COMPLEMENTARY COLOURS Some colours are used by artists to help or 'complement' others, and it is useful to know which hues can be most satisfactorily associated. You will probably have noticed already that Victorian landscape painters had a habit of including a figure in a bright red coat or dress in any landscape that was predominantly green. They did this deliberately, knowing that the small quantity of red they had introduced would add an extra piquancy and brilliance to the contrasting green.

As a guide that will help you to select other pairs of complementary colours satisfactorily, it is helpful to be able to reproduce a 'colour circle', like the one shown in Illustration 17. Red is directly opposite green, you will notice, and blue is directly opposite yellow. A small amount of yellow in a predominantly blue picture will probably be just about as valuable as a small amount of blue in a yellow picture.

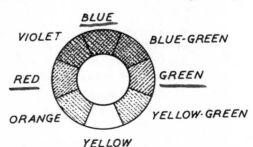

17. The colour circle, in a very much simplified version

Let us think for a moment of how such a colour circle can be used. Let us suppose you are painting a picture that is pitched almost exclusively in tones of brown. Let us suppose that the picture seems rather lifeless, and that you think it needs a little extra 'something', to lift it, and give it more vitality. Brown is a shade of red, or red mixed with black, as you will know if you have carried out the experiments already described in this chapter. The tonic your picture needs is, therefore, a little green, either pure, or 'adulterated' with black or white, or both. Add this, and you will be using your theoretical knowledge of complementary colours in a thoroughly practical way.

WARM AND COOL COLOURS   There is a certain amount of disagreement among painters about the warmth (or otherwise) of the various colours on the palette. The general consensus of opinion seems to be that orange, red and crimson are warm colours, and that yellow-green, green and blue-green are cool colours. Colours that fall in these two categories are generally used in opposition to each other—that is to say, a warm light will tend to produce cool shadows and a cool light will tend to produce warm shadows. When you are painting—for example—a head, you will be able to produce an accentuated effect of solidity if you use on the well-lit planes colours drawn from the warm side of the colour circle and on the shaded planes cool tones of blue, blue-green and blue-grey. Paul Cézanne was one of the first painters to exploit the contrast between warm and cool colours in a fully significant way. Look at the broad, domed forehead in one of his self-portraits and you will find it as instructive, from the point of view of colour theory, as any chapter in a textbook.

DISCORDS   Why do some combinations of colours seem to set our teeth on edge? A bright orange scarf thrown on hastily by a girl in a hurry may 'clash', as people say, with her salmon pink dress so aggressively that sensitive people will not be able to notice the shape of either, or her personal attractiveness. Discords of this kind are usually due to some distortion in the tonal relationships of the colours. Salmon pink, for instance, is a tint of scarlet, which, in the order of the spectrum, is slightly darker than orange. By reducing the intensity of the scarlet, and by lightening it in tone, to produce pink, the natural order is disturbed and our sense of sight gets a considerable shock.

Not all discords are undesirable, of course. Some of the most memorable colour schemes contain factors that would be in larger quantities or under different circumstances quite overpowering. The use of colour is an extremely personal business—it will be up to you to develop your own individual tastes by constant invention and experiment.

COLOURS THAT ESTABLISH A MOOD   To many artists, each colour in the spectrum seems to have its own particular character and to be indispensable in evoking a particular mood. A picture of a deserted street in a windswept industrial town might be carried out by one artist entirely in tints and shades of blue. A study of a dense wood in midsummer might well be painted almost exclusively in rich greens, or in shades of orange. Pablo Picasso's 'Blue Period' has been mentioned before. The paintings carried out by that great artist during his early days in Paris supply some splendid examples of the potent effects of a strictly limited colour scheme. It is unlikely that the urban beggars, blind men and impoverished drinkers he depicted would move us emotionally one quarter so much if they were portrayed in the pure bright colours we associate with a seaside carnival.

SIX

KEEPING A SKETCHBOOK

When we get up in the morning we wash, dress ourselves, tidy our hair, brush our teeth and start our day in a way that is largely dictated by habit. We have done these things so many times before that we no longer have to devote a lot of thought to the mechanical side of our preparations. In exactly the same way, an artist who keeps a sketchbook and makes a habit of recording anything he sees that interests him will soon cease to be worried by the purely technical problems of drawing. The task of reducing a three-dimensional vista into a two-dimensional image is a considerable one, and presents great difficulties to the beginner. If you can make sketching a habit, you will soon find that the difficulties are lessened, as they are for the professional artist. Practice makes perfect in the Fine Arts, as it does in so many other human activities.

One of the first essentials, then, will be to have a sketchbook and a pen or pencil by you, always—and ready for action. It is quite paralysing to have to search for materials when the need to make a drawing becomes suddenly urgent.

All shops that sell artists' materials stock sketchbooks in a wide variety of shapes and sizes. You can buy one of these if you like—the students' sketchbooks made up of scores of sheets of thin bond paper are ideal—or you can make for yourself a looseleaf pocketbook, into which you can put any clean pieces of scrap paper that come into your possession. If you strip the pages out of an old discarded hard-cover book of a suitable size, and paste or glue retaining flaps to the boards as shown in Illustration 18, you will have a sketchbook that is useful, commodious, and that can be easily replaced when it is worn or over-soiled.

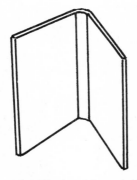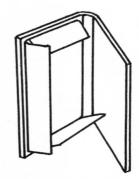

18. This shows how the boards of an unwanted book (left)
can be fitted with flaps to make a useful sketchbook

DRAWING PEOPLE Learning to draw figures is often regarded as the hardest part of an artist's training—people move
about so unpredictably, their bodies are so complex, their
expressions so fleeting and subtle. But even a beginner can
tackle figure drawing profitably if there is no need for him—or
her—to show the resulting sketches to anyone else. Keep your
early efforts secret and you will be able to work in a free, uninhibited way. No one will be able to laugh at your drawings,
or criticise them, unless you ask for guidance.

Suppose that you are watching an old fisherman sitting on
a low wall, and that you have a sketchbook and a pencil or
pen handy. The first thing you will want to do is to realise, on
your paper, a simplified version of the main forms that make
up the fisherman. If you start at the top and work downwards,
as so many beginners do, depicting the head in the most meticulous way, then the neck, then the shoulders, and so on you
will almost certainly find by the time you have reached the
feet that the various parts do not 'hang together', as artists
say—the fisherman on your paper may not resemble the fisherman sitting on the wall in the slightest degree. The fisherman

51

may be no longer on the wall, anyway, by that time, for detailed part-by-part drawing can only be an extremely slow process. No, it is much better to draft in roughly the whole figure as soon as you start to sketch, remembering the old saying that a drawing should always be complete 'as far as it goes'.

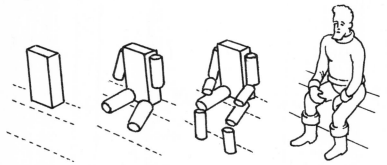

19. Don't be defeated by the difficulty of drawing a figure in the correct proportion. Tackle it in easy stages, like this

Illustration 19 shows the stages by which you might well rough in the main forms of the old fisherman we have been talking about. First, his torso or trunk is put down in the simplest possible terms, almost as if it is a matchbox or a packing case—this 'distillation' helps you to establish the inclination and proportion of the torso in the very easiest way.

Then the thighs and upper arms are added, very much as if they are simple cylinders. You may notice—if you experiment a little with your own body—that the upper arm is approximately two-thirds the length of the torso, while the thigh, which contains the longest single bone in the human body, the femur, would prove very nearly as long as the torso if the knee were pressed up to the shoulder.

Then the forearms and lower parts of the legs are added—again, in a drastically simplified way. You will notice that

52

each of these is a little shorter than the upper part of the same limb. The lower part of the arm, which is given its length by the radius and ulna bones, is an inch or two shorter than the upper part in all normal people. The lower part of the leg, which contains the nearly straight tibia and fibula bones, is shorter than the thigh in the approximate proportion 6 : 5. Remember simple facts like that about proportion and a lot of your sketching problems will be solved.

In the last drawing, you will see how the head, hands, feet and clothes can be added to the tentatively drawn 'puppet figure', giving it a certain amount of life and reality. If your eyes travel rapidly between the subject you are drawing and the paper you are drawing on each stroke of your pencil will add something to the general impression of truth. There is no real substitute, in the final stages of a drawing, for an urgent sense of enquiry.

DRAWING MOVING PEOPLE   An old fisherman might sit still on a wall for a very few minutes, but it is highly unlikely that most of the people you will want to draw will be so obliging. That is why the word 'movement' plays so important a part in an artist's vocabulary. It is applied to the barely perceptible inclinations of a still figure as freely as to the twists and turns of an active person. If you want every figure you draw to be really convincing, you should try to notice the rhythmical flow of the body and limbs. Look at the subtle movements that are made to restore the balance of a figure when—say—an arm is raised or a knee is turned outwards. Examine the relative positions of the sternum (the breast bone, that forms the central link in the shoulder girdle) and the feet. Put a straight edge— metaphorically speaking—across the shoulders and a straight edge across the hips of anybody you are sketching and see how closely they are aligned. You cannot draw a figure satisfactorily by just copying the outlines.

DRAWING PLACES Landscape drawing and painting will be dealt with more fully in Chapter Eleven, but it may be appropriate to include here a brief note about the kind of sketch you will probably want to make when you are travelling somewhere—when there is no time to set up an easel and embark on a thoroughly considered composition. In such hurried circumstances you will find a viewfinder a great help. Cut a square or rectangular hole in a piece of cardboard, hold it up so that only the subject that interests you is visible and all the irrelevant surroundings hidden, and try to reproduce in your sketchbook the main shapes—and the main shapes only —in the view before you. Simplified into a few broad areas of tone, the subject will be relatively manageable, and you will be able to develop in more detail any part that is particularly important, so that it becomes a focal point, or what artists call 'the centre of interest'.

JUDGING PROPORTION One of the most difficult problems you will come up against while you are learning to draw is the problem of proportion. Unless you can judge correctly the relationship between the height, the width and the thickness of any person or object you are drawing, you will find it impossible to make your representation of that person or object look really convincing. It is harder to make a drawing of a brick look exactly like a drawing of a brick—and not like a drawing of a matchbox—than one might imagine.

Have you ever seen an artist hold up a pencil at arm's length and move his thumb backwards and forwards on it until he has seemed to take some exact measurement? Well, that is just what he has been doing—he has been cutting off, along the shank of the pencil, one of the main dimensions of the subject he is drawing, so that he can compare it with one of the other main dimensions. He has not been measuring in inches—that would be virtually impossible—but in some other strictly

54

relative unit of length. He may have discovered—say—that the width of his subject is exactly one third of its height, and that its thickness is exactly one half of its width. That discovery will have helped him to construct a recognisable image of his subject on his paper more rapidly and more inevitably than any slavishly accurate copying of its silhouette. So, don't be afraid to hold out a pencil at arm's length—and at right angles to your line of vision—if you want to be an accurate draughtsman, or draughtswoman, in the good old-fashioned way.

UPRIGHTS Another factor you will have to bear in mind when you are sketching is the verticality (or otherwise) of all upright lines, and the pitch—if any—of all approximately horizontal lines. If you find this difficult to understand, let us imagine that you are drawing a house, and that the house has a very simple form, like that of a great big cube. All the upright arrises, or corners, will be exactly vertical, won't they? If the house has been built correctly, and is still structurally sound, a dropped penny should fall parallel to each of them without hitting the brickwork or veering away from it. Therefore, you should be able to plot those lines on your paper without too much difficulty by referring constantly to the paper's upright sides—unless, that is, you are seeing the building from a particularly close viewpoint so that the perspective is grotesquely distorted. In all ordinary circumstances it is helpful to hold up a 'plumb line'—a piece of cotton or string with a weight on the end—that will act as a check on all uprights and show you where, if anywhere, there are any misleading deviants.

LINEAR PERSPECTIVE How much will you need to know about linear perspective before you go out sketching? That is a question that may be worrying you, as it has worried so

55

many thousands of people before you—and understandably, for many lengthy volumes have been written about the theory of linear perspective without exhausting the possibilities of the subject. But there are only two or three simple basic facts you will have to know if you are to be able to sort out most of the tangle for yourself.

(1.)   The first of these facts concerns <u>the strange behaviour of parallel lines that recede from the spectator towards the hori-zon</u>—they meet, in case it has never been demonstrated to you, *VP* at an imaginary point opposite the spectator's eye known usually to artists as the 'Vanishing Point'. You will almost certainly have noticed that the parallel sides of a road, or of a river, appear to get closer as they pass into the distance. Their ulti-mate conjunction (demonstrated in Illustration 20) is one of the easiest results of the workings of perspective to understand.

20. All the lines that meet at the horizon in this illustration would be parallel to each other in real life

But what happens if the road (or river) turns inconsiderately to the left or right? Not many roads or rivers are, literally, 'dead straight' in any part of the world. The answer to that question is most easily demonstrated by another drawing.

Illustration 21 shows how a second Vanishing Point comes into existence almost as if by magic as soon as the parallel sides of the road shown in Illustration 20 change direction. If the road swings to the right, the new Vanishing Point appears to the right of the original point. If the road swings to the left, the new Vanishing Point appears to the left of the original point. It's as simple to remember as that.

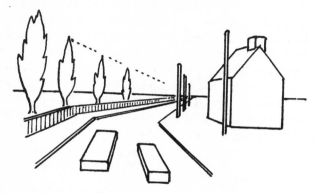

21. This shows what happens if a road swings sharply to the right

And, if the road goes uphill, what then? Once again, a single drawing is worth pages of verbal description. Illustration 22 shows how a road with parallel sides, and with fences to right and left, appears to produce an extra Vanishing Point, immediately above the original point, as soon as part of the road is inclined at a steep enough angle for the change of plane to be perceptible. If you want to draw a road in undulating country that twists to right and left, as well as leading the traveller up and down, you may have to plot as many as a dozen different Vanishing Points, and use every one of them, before you can produce the required effect.

Before you can plot a Vanishing Point above (or below) the

horizon, you will have to know exactly where the horizon is. That may seem obvious, but it is surprising how many artists will start to draw or paint a complicated landscape or townscape without considering their eye level, and without deciding where, on their paper or canvas, the horizon will fall. If you are drawing an actual scene, on the spot, and if the horizon is hidden—by buildings, possibly, or trees—you can always do a bit of detective work by holding a straight edge up so that it coincides with one of the receding straight lines in the scene before you. If, then, you extend this line upwards, or downwards, and if you do exactly the same with a line that is in real life parallel to it you will be able to locate a Vanishing Point, and, therefore, the horizon that passes through it, where the two extensions cross. Illustration 23 shows how this method could be employed to find the horizon in a landscape where it would otherwise be totally obscured.

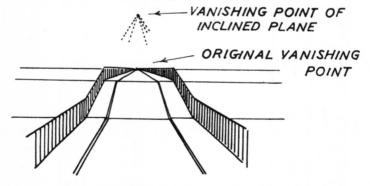

22. An extra Vanishing Point is needed when a level road suddenly becomes an uphill slope

GROWTH Plants, shrubs, bushes and trees play so great a part in the make-up of the world around us that it is important for us to be able to draw and paint them convincingly. A slight knowledge of the elements of botany is useful for any artist,

58

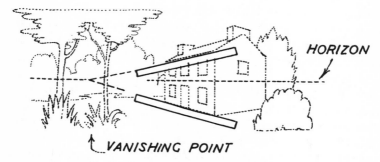

23. A simple way of locating a hidden horizon

but even if you have never studied the growth of natural forms
scientifically you can soon learn to penetrate, even in the thick
conditions of high summer, the obscuring shrouds of lush
foliage that appeal to superficial observers, and to see the simple
flowing forms that are so impressive to us all in the cold bare
light of December.

And that's as valuable a way to start as any. When you are
faced with a landscape that contains a lot of fluffy greenery,
look out for, and draw, only those parts of it that would be
there in mid-winter. Each kind of tree sends up its own,
entirely individual kind of trunk, and its branches will grow
from that trunk in an exactly characteristic way. Begin, then,
by drawing the main stem, and as you work along study how
all the subordinate members grow out of it, and away from it—
whether they grow upwards like the branches of a poplar,
horizontally like the branches of many conifers, or downwards
like the branches of a weeping beech or willow. The main
masses of foliage can be added afterwards, being considered
primarily as solid forms and not as superficial textures. If you
don't understand how some thousands of thin light leaves
can make up one solid form look at the landscape paintings
of Paul Cézanne. Some of his trees look as though they have

been built up with lumps of coloured concrete—and they are none the worse for this monumental solidity. It gives them an appearance of reality that is often totally absent from the trees in the paintings of lesser men.

DRAWING ANIMALS   Animals are just as interesting to draw as trees—and as difficult. Few animals will keep still for long enough for us to draw them, unless we happen to catch them asleep, or penned so tightly in cages or market places that they appear to lose temporarily all the vitality that makes them so attractive. Even a grazing sheep or cow will lift up its head and move off disconcertingly if it senses that its services as a model have been taken for granted.

Stuffed animals—especially the fine specimens to be seen in many of our museums—probably provide the best facilities for prolonged study, since we can scrutinise them at leisure and from a number of different viewpoints, and we can, if necessary, cause extra light to be thrown on them where more illumination is needed. Of course, a drawing of a stuffed animal is always liable to look rather lifeless, however careful the taxidermist may have been. It will be up to you—if you try to make some sketches of 'permanently suspended animation'—to look for, and stress, the lines that remind you of the energy once so characteristic of your subject. Don't get bogged down in a mass of insignificant surface detail. It won't help your drawing at all to include every hair, every feather or every scale.

If there is any danger of your becoming over-fussy and 'narrow', take a sketchbook out and draw every live animal you can see, without caring whether your drawings will be worth looking at, eventually, or not (the chances are that they will be much more lively and instructive if you are working unselfconsciously). Try to catch the 'movement' of the animal you are drawing in the simplest possible way—the little sketch on the left of Illustration 24, for instance, would serve as a useful start for the slightly more developed drawing of a horse on the right. Be prepared to stop work on a drawing as soon as an animal has moved toc radically from the position you have been studying, and as soon as your memories of it have faded. It may be tantalising to have a number of half-completed scrawls in your sketchbook, but they will be far more vital, and valuable, than a smaller number that have been cobbled up with a little forced invention.

24. With a few lines, boldly drawn, you can catch the essential 'movement' of an animal more satisfactorily than you can with a mass of fussy detail

THE WORLD AROUND US   No one is too poor, or too mean, or too drab to be of interest to some artist, somewhere. No surroundings can ever be so tedious that they are completely without pictorial possibilities. Rembrandt and Picasso found some of their most historically memorable models among the derelict paupers who haunted the neighbourhood of their studios. Daumier discovered visual drama in the dry-as-dust atmosphere of the law courts. Toulouse-Lautrec explored the graphic possibilities of the brothel, the midnight café and the circus. Walter Richard Sickert immortalised on canvas the tawdry décor of various cheap Camden Town lodging houses, and planned some of the most exciting paintings that have been conceived in this century in the garish, tumbledown music halls of the East End. Augustus John 'went on the road'

61

with gypsies and tinkers. Rich, colourful surroundings are not essential for the really great artist. The master takes glamour with him wherever he goes.

Look at Illustration 25 and you will see the kind of sketch one of these great artists—Toulouse-Lautrec—habitually made when he was 'relaxing', or stocking up his storehouse of visual memories (with him, the two were almost synonymous). As you will notice, the lady and the greyhound in the sketch

25. When a great artist wishes to record some scene that has attracted his attention he is not afraid to simplify

have been recorded with a few bold, decisive strokes that seem to have distilled the whole meaning from the complex scene in front of the artist. You, too, can extract the essence of the visible world with your pencil or pen if you are prepared to open your eyes, to forget all preconceived ideas and prejudices, and to put down on paper with speed and humility the many good things that can present themselves to you in a single hour of completely whole-hearted *observing*. You will have to live every minute to the full if you want to develop as an artist.

SEVEN

WATER COLOUR PAINTING

Are you the sort of person who enjoys doing a difficult job really well, who can sit back after a long struggle with intractable materials and sigh with pleasure at the final accomplishment? If you are, you will probably find that water colour painting appeals to you as much as any other kind, for it is a form of art that depends on patience, technical skill and a sincere love of craftsmanship. That's why true water colour painting is so rare today, when patience is at a discount, technical skill in the Fine Arts is seldom striven for, and craftsmanship all too often goes unnoticed. Oil paintings are collected by a great many people—water colours are collected by only a few connoisseurs.

WATER COLOUR MATERIALS

Paper: Special papers are prepared and sold for water colour painting, and you will have to invest in a few sheets at least of a suitable type if you are going to achieve satisfactory results. You can draw and sketch in pencil or ink on discarded leaves from old scribbling pads, but water colours demand the same kind of consideration as a spoiled child—they only want the best!

Among the many excellent water colour papers marketed today are Whatman or Arnold papers, which should only be purchased in the lighter grades, and with a smooth or moderately smooth surface; Michallet papers, which are rather slighter, and do not allow quite so much rubbing and scrubbing; and David Cox papers, which demand direct, unhesitating workmanship and are, perhaps, more suited for experienced craftsmen than beginners.

63

You will probably be offered toned and lightly coloured papers when you go shopping for water colour painting materials, but do not be tempted to buy them until you have had a great deal of experience. For one thing, they give a misleading air of quality even to the slightest and most vaporous sketch, and, for another, they cut out by their very nature the use of all pure whites unless those whites are superimposed by the addition of thick, opaque body colours, which will spoil the true, beautiful water colour surface you will be trying so hard to achieve.

You will probably be offered 'water colour sketching blocks', too, which, although compact and convenient, should be refused. As will be explained later, water colour washes can only be laid smoothly and satisfactorily on sheets of paper that have been suitably stretched. The sheets of paper that are quite loosely combined to make up these blocks tend to warp and belly when work is carried out on the surfaces above them. By the time you have used the top half of a block you will probably find that the lower sheets are quite useless, and only fit for the waste paper basket.

To stretch a sheet of water colour paper most satisfactorily it should be some two or three inches larger, in each direction, than the drawing board on which it is to be strained. Damp it thoroughly, and bend the edges over on to the sides or back of the board, pinning them firmly in place with large drawing pins when you have pulled the paper as tight as you possibly can without tearing it. When the stretched paper has dried, it will present a temptingly flat and brilliant surface for you to work on. This method is shown on the left of Illustration 26.

If you are only able to obtain (or afford) sheets of paper that are the same size as, or smaller than, the board you are going to work on, you can use gummed tape instead of drawing pins to hold the edges while the moisture dries out. This method is shown on the right of Illustration 26.

Good drawing is the basis of most fine painting. An unknown artist of the Lombard School has caught with unerring accuracy the supple grace of these two cheetahs, or hunting leopards *(Trustees of the British Museum)*

Both these fine water colours, of Greta Bridge, ABOVE, and of a mountain pass in the Tyrol, are by John Sell Cotman (1782-1842). Notice how the artist eliminated much unnecessary detail and reduced the complex landscapes he was studying to a few areas of correctly related tone
(Trustees of the British Museum)

This beautiful painting of hollyhocks and other flowers is by Jan van Huijsum. Much of the charm of this small masterpiece is due to the meticulous care with which the tiniest details have been observed and recorded *(Trustees of the National Gallery, London)*

Compare the free, spontaneous handling of this portrait of a shrimp girl by William Hogarth with the studied grandeur of the portrait by Rembrandt *(Trustees of the National Gallery, London)*

Here is Rembrandt's 'Margaretha de Geer, Wife of Jacob Trip', one of the most profound studies ever made by this prince of painters *(Trustees of the National Gallery, London)*

Figures can often be used to add interest and vitality to a landscape. Here are, RIGHT, John Crome's 'The Poringland Oak' (*Trustees of the Tate Gallery, London*),and, BELOW, Richard Wilson's 'Holt Bridge, the River Dee' (*Trustees of the National Gallery, London*)

Two twentieth-century artists who have exploited the pictorial possibilities of buildings are L. S. Lowry, 'The Pond', ABOVE *(Trustees of the Tate Gallery, London)*, and L. Pissarro, 'Effects of Snow' *(Trustees of the National Gallery, London)*

Skilful use of unusual geological features can make a picture extremely dramatic. So can intense lighting from a single source. Here are
examples of both — James Ward's 'Gordale Scar, Yorkshire', ABOVE,
and 'An Experiment with the Air Pump', by Joseph Wright of Derby
(Trustees of the Tate Gallery, London)

Only a great artist can show the sun in his pictures without courting disaster.
Here are two famous canvases in which the golden radiance of sunshine is
shown with subtlety and truth. ABOVE, 'The *Fighting Temeraire* Towed to
Her Last Berth', by Turner. BELOW, 'The Château de Steen', by Rubens
(Trustees of the National Gallery, London)

Lakes and rivers make fascinating subjects for the artist. Here are pictures of Venice, by Francesco Guardi *(Trustees of the National Gallery, London)*, and of the Thames at Chiswick, by Victor Pasmore *(Trustees of the Tate Gallery, London)*

Long hours of careful still-life study enabled Harold Gilman to make this brilliant picture of Mrs. Mounter at the breakfast table *(Trustees of the Tate Gallery, London, and the artist's widow)*

Flowers and gardens evoke a sympathetic response from all of us. Who could resist this beautiful painting of a Shoreham garden by Samuel Palmer? *(Victoria and Albert Museum, Crown Copyright)*

26. Two methods of stretching water colour paper to obtain
a good working surface

Brushes: Red or black sable brushes can be used for water colour painting, and those with round ferrules are undoubtedly the best. Don't buy too many brushes at first. Equip yourself with three or four medium size brushes (say, a No. 6, a No. 8, a No. 10 and a No. 12) and get to know the capabilities of each. All water colour brushes should be washed out thoroughly after use and left to dry *in a point*. A brush put away carelessly, with its bristles clogged up with pigment, may never be the same again.

Paints: Water colours are marketed in two different ways—in dry cakes, and moist and ready for use, in tubes. Obviously, where speed is essential—as, for example, when fleeting atmospheric effects are being recorded—tube colours have a certain advantage, but in spite of this many artists prefer old-fashioned colour boxes, where all the pigments are visible and immediately accessible, and where no caps have to be screwed on or off. It seems a sensible course of action to experiment with both types of colour before you settle down to use one kind exclusively.

65

The range of colours available to the water colourist is almost as extensive as that offered to the painter in oils, and every artist has to find his—or her—ideal palette after a certain amount of experiment. Among the colours that are most generally useful, as well as being reasonably permanent, are the following:

Yellow ochre: A charming colour, both when it is used by itself and when it is mixed with ivory black or with various blues to make the rich, medium or subtle greens needed for landscape painting.

Aureolin: A brighter yellow, but one that may not be quite so stable when it is mixed with some other colours, such as crimson lake.

Light red: A permanent and comparatively powerful colour, which can be mixed with yellow and blue to produce some warm and beautiful neutral greys. Unlike more vivid hues, light red can be used freely with the recommended blues without producing any of the virulent lilacs and purples that bedevil the paintings of so many inept colourists.

Cyanine blue, or *Leitch's blue:* This is probably one of the most beautiful and useful blues that is at the same time reasonably permanent. French ultramarine, or French blue, is permanent, but it does not produce in mixture such subtle or attractive greens. Antwerp blue is a charming colour, but it cannot be guaranteed to last.

Ivory black: Used alone, or with minute admixtures of other colours, ivory black will produce some really beautiful neutral tones, the warmth or coolness of a shadow being suggested by the amount of blue or red that is allowed to exert its influence. Don't be tempted to use ivory black—or any dark colour, for that matter—so thickly that it resembles an opaque body colour. It will only retain its beautifully limpid quality if the whiteness of the underlying paper is allowed to play some part in the final effect.

66

Viridian, or *Transparent green oxide of chromium:* This is a rich and powerful green that the paint manufacturers claim is absolutely permanent and unfading. Its chief drawback is its potency—how many of us can resist the temptation to splash really strong vivid colours around when we are trying to capture the warm luxuriance of a summer landscape, for example?

Burnt sienna: This attractive earth brown will play a very versatile and useful part in any colour box, and is dark enough to be used alone as a 'monochrome' when a tone sketch is needed.

You will be able to produce some very exciting and decorative paintings with those seven water colours alone, and you would be well advised, in fact, to explore some of their almost infinite possibilities before you extend your range. When you are ready to add further colours, you may find that some of these suit your particular style, and colour sense:

French ultramarine, or *French blue:* A comparatively cheap substitute for the dramatically expensive 'genuine ultramarine', which is made from lapis lazuli. French ultramarine is almost as powerful as viridian, and has to be used, like that colour, with discretion.

Raw sienna: Some useful and attractive additions to the range of available browns can be made by the purchase of this pleasant earth colour.

Rose madder: A beautifully rich colour, capable of producing, with other colours, a variety of tints and shades which range from the subtlest warm greys to the most luscious of deep wine-reds. The artificially produced substitutes rose madder (alizarin) and alizarin crimson are cheaper, and useful, but they will not produce colours that are quite as sumptuous as those yielded by the genuine madder root.

Light red, Payne's grey and *Naples yellow* also have their admirers.

67

THE TECHNIQUE OF WATER COLOUR PAINTING The correct way to apply water colours to a ready-stretched piece of paper can probably be best described if two examples of working method are cited—one good, and one bad.

In the first example, a brush is charged with colour that has been carefully mixed and diluted with water in a clean china palette, and then the colour is washed quickly and plentifully on to the area to be tinted, guided with the brush tip to the required edges, and then left undisturbed. No part of the painted area is traversed by the brush more than once, and the colour is free to dry out slowly, very much as an unnoticed blot might dry if it had fallen by chance on the same piece of paper. An area coloured in this way will possess an incomparably fresh and transparent quality, and should have the lovely soft peach-skin-like patina known to most artists as 'bloom'.

In the second example, a brush is charged with colour in exactly the same way, but this time the artist is not working methodically. He tints the required area with colour, drains some away before it is dry by dipping into it the hair-tips of a slightly moist brush, and then tries to build up its intensity by superimposing a second coat over the first. The paint surface that results from this laboured application will almost certainly be opaque and lacking in freshness and vitality. The 'bloom' noticed in the first example won't be there. So, if you want your work to have the very special quality that is most prized in fine water colours you will just have to learn to paint as directly as you can, with a minimum of second thoughts and second coats.

Sometimes—as, for example, when you want to paint a sky, a calm sea or a wide field—you will need to cover a very large area of paper with a smooth, thin coat of transparent colour, or what is known as a 'wash'. Laying a wash is quite a simple task once you have had a bit of practice. This is how it is done:

68

First, mix up the main colour and any subsidiary colours you may wish to introduce into it in the course of your wash-laying (a sky may be quite a rich blue near the zenith, for example, and a comparatively pale pink by the horizon). Use plenty of water, and make sure that you have mixed up enough colour, with some over to spare. There will be no time to stop and mix up more once the wash is on the paper.

Then take your drawing board on your knee (easels are very rarely used by water colour painters) and tip it to a reasonably steep angle.

If a wash is being laid satisfactorily, the slope of the paper should be sufficient to carry all surplus moisture and pigment to the lowest edge of a painted strip, but it should not be so acute that unwanted runnels of paint detach themselves from the main body and run chaotically downhill. You may have to do a bit of rapid adjustment before you find the most suitable angle.

Then start painting at the top of the area to be covered, drawing the brush horizontally across the paper as shown in Illustration 27. Each stroke of the brush should release the paint that has collected along the lower edge of the paper

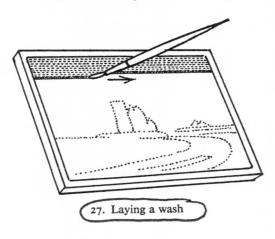

27. Laying a wash

covered by the last stroke, so that a fresh band is covered each time. Don't turn back and retouch any part of the painted surface if you can possibly help it. If you do, you will almost certainly spoil the lovely unity of surface you are trying to achieve.

When you have covered any part of the area to be coloured, squeeze the surplus moisture gently from your brush by pulling it slowly through your fingers, then suck the surplus moisture from the paper by touching the paint near the lowest edge with the tip of the brush.

Not all paintings consist of large unbroken areas of colour, of course. To keep different colours in adjacent smaller areas from running into each other, you can leave an extremely thin strip of white paper between them, if you are really dexterous. This strip can be 'filled in' with either of the adjoining colours when the paper surface is sufficiently dry to allow it.

Sometimes, you will find that an area you have painted is too dark in tone, and appears to spoil your picture. To reduce a dark, let it dry thoroughly, then wash a very little absolutely clean water over it. As soon as the paint surface has been thoroughly re-moistened, rub it carefully with a dry, clean, cotton rag. This will remove much of the paint and leave a patina that has its own individual attractiveness.

TRADITIONAL (AND OTHER) METHODS There have been times in the history of painting when water colour work has flourished exceedingly, and there have been other times when the deliberate techniques it involves have seemed unrewarding and have fallen out of favour. When water colour painting was in its zenith in the great days of Paul Sandby, Thomas Girtin, John Sell Cotman and Peter de Wint, most of the devoted practitioners of the fashionable medium followed some rarely varied procedures when they were building up a picture.

First, they would 'realise' the sky and the further distance, using only the thinnest washes of the palest and most transparent blues. The 'air tint', this was often called.

Then, they would construct the area known as the 'middle distance', which, to lead the eye well into the picture, would usually contain a castle or some other notable building, a lake, or perhaps a picturesque ruin. This middle distance would be painted in a pale ochre, a faint sienna, a suggestion of umber or some other well-watered-down brown.

Finally, they would add the foreground, using strong tones of brown or black, reinforced with suggestions of colour— as, for example, some green in a tree or assorted hues in a group of figures or animals.

Their procedure, having the inevitability of routine, aroused no fierce criticism, but as it forced them to choose subjects where the terrain could be neatly subdivided into the three main zones just described, it was somewhat restricting.

You, too, can adopt that or some entirely personal system of building up a water colour painting if it suits you to work in a regularly methodical way. If you prefer, you can be entirely unconventional in the way you use water colours—you can use them to reinforce pen and ink sketches most effectively or you can use them in conjunction with body colours in a way that would have horrified the purists of the early nineteenth century. As was said earlier in this book, when you are learning to paint you should not be bound too rigidly by rules. Experiment freely, and you will find that the wide experience that results will give you the best instruction of all.

71

EIGHT

PAINTING IN OILS

Oil painting has a history so long and distinguished that for many people other forms of painting simply do not exist! The greatest masterpieces of Titian, Rembrandt, Rubens, Reynolds and Gainsborough—to name but a few artists whose works are admired all over the world—were carried out almost exclusively with oil-bound pigments. Once you have tried oil colours and discovered their amazing flexibility and subtlety you will know exactly why they commended themselves so compulsively to so many of the masters. Tempera colours must have seemed very stiff and hard to manage after the new medium was introduced towards the end of the fifteenth century.

Although it is not possible to start painting in oils without a certain amount of outlay on colours and other materials these need not be unduly expensive if a little discretion is used. Obviously, it is to the advantage of the trade to suggest that a certain number of 'borderline' requirements are absolutely essential. In this chapter, the emphasis will be on simplicity. You can always add more items to your basic equipment if—and when —you feel inclined to be lavish.

COLOURS, GENERALLY   The way to find out about colours most satisfactorily is, of course, to use them. Only after a little practical experience will you find out whether 'artists' quality' finely ground colours are worth—to you—the small amount more than students' colours they will cost. You will learn, too, which colours—such as Prussian blue—have plenty of 'body' or power, and can, therefore, be bought in comparatively small quantities. You will learn which colours—such as Venetian red—are comparatively opaque, and will cover other colours satisfactorily, and which are transparent, lending themselves to glazing and staining. To start your researches, here are suggestions for a minimal basic palette in which all the colours are compatible. Pigments—like the members of some families—do not always agree when they are mixed together without some consideration of their separate natures.

WHITE Don't stint yourself when you are buying white paint—buy as large a tube as you can afford. The quality of your work may be seriously impaired if you have to thin out your paint with oil or turpentine and its surface then resembles the sparse, washy patina of a water colour.

Titanium white is probably the best of the three white paints most usually offered for sale. It is brilliant, non-poisonous, inert and no more expensive than flake white or zinc white in most art materials dealers' catalogues.

Flake white or '*white lead*' has had a long and mixed history. Many artists prefer it to any other, since it forms as it dries a tough, leathery skin which can stand up to a great deal of punishment without cracking or peeling. It is poisonous, though, especially if it is being handled in powder form; it tends to turn yellow if it is stored in a dark place; and it cannot be mixed with French ultramarine, cobalt violet or any of the natural madders with a full guarantee of permanence. In spite of these drawbacks, it is popular. You may have to try both flake white and titanium white before you decide which you prefer.

Zinc white is a third alternative. It is a slow drier, and it does not form as tough a skin as flake white, but it can be mixed with French ultramarine without making the blue fugitive, and it is safe and pleasant to handle.

YELLOW The best yellow to use in a strictly limited palette is probably *yellow ochre*, which is one of the safe, cheap earth colours mentioned in Chapter Five. (The other earth colours —raw and burnt sienna, raw and burnt umber, Venetian red, Indian red and light red—make sound additions to any palette, veering as they do towards red and brown.) Yellow ochre is not particularly bright, though. If you want brilliance, you will have to add or substitute *lemon yellow*, which is reasonably permanent, or *cadmium yellow*, which, having a slight tendency towards orange, is not quite so useful for mixing greens.

RED   *Light red*, mentioned above, is a cheap, reliable earth colour, and is probably as good as any for a strictly limited palette. If you think it too dull for your requirements you can choose one of these:

Cadmium red or *cadmium scarlet*: These are both brilliant and reasonably permanent colours, but they should only be bought in well-known brands, as cheaper pigments have occasionally been substituted by unscrupulous traders.

Alizarin scarlet and *alizarin crimson*: These too are attractive and useful colours, but they are not suitable if ultramarine is to find a place on your palette as there is a basic incompatibility here.

Vermilion is one of the brightest reds you can obtain, but it has to be used with great care. Being usually made from some form of mercuric sulphide it can be converted all too readily by impurities in the atmosphere into other compounds which are black and unsightly.

BLUE   If you can only include one blue in a basic palette there is a strong case for choosing *cobalt*. It is not a very intense colour and it is rather expensive, but it can be used for mixing quite rich greens, which is more than can be said for *French blue*, or *French ultramarine*. This inclines to be purplish in hue, as it is supplied by most manufacturers. Ideally, you should include two blues if you can—French ultramarine (real ultramarine is fantastically expensive) for mixing with reds to produce purples and violets; and *Prussian blue*, for mixing with yellows to produce the really sonorous greens you will need when you are painting landscapes.

GREEN   *Viridian* or *transparent green oxide of chromium* is a lovely rich green and has largely replaced the more subtle green earth *terre verte*.

BLACK   You read earlier that white should be purchased in bulk and used freely if your work is not to look thin and meagre. In the same way, black should be used sparingly if it is not to creep in an unwelcome fashion into all your pure hues and tints and make them look grey and dirty.

Used to produce strong, dramatically dark tones, black can perform a most valuable function. You can choose between *lamp black*, which is quite a quick drier, *ivory black*, which is rather slower, and *blue black*, which, mixed with white, will give you some splendidly soft silky greys. PAYNE'S GREY

VEHICLES   Nowadays, most artists' oil colours are sold in tubes, and they are nearly always ground in plenty of poppy oil, which, being a very slow drier, is intended to prevent the paints solidifying while they are still in the shop or colour box, and before they are in their right places on a canvas. If you want your paintings to dry without inconvenient delay you will be well advised to extract some of this surplus vehicle with ordinary blotting paper, replacing it, when you are ready to paint, with one of these:

Linseed oil: This is one of the best known and most frequently used vehicles, and has been for a very long time. Unfortunately, it has certain drawbacks. Paint mixed with linseed oil quickly forms a 'skin', but it may not harden right through for more than a year. If further coats are placed on top before

75

the underlying layers are hard, the oil may be absorbed from them as though by blotting paper, and this can cause cracking and other mishaps. A mixture of linseed oil and turpentine, in equal parts, is recommended by some instructors.

Turpentine: When you are starting to paint in oils, you may find a 'thin' spirit or essence such as turpentine or gasoline more satisfactory as a vehicle than a fatty oil like linseed. Turpentine is sold in various grades ranging from the cheap 'turpentine substitutes' which often contain harmful impurities to the comparatively expensive purified essences that are prepared specially for artists. It is usually fairly easy to find a reasonably pure grade that is not prohibitively expensive at a drug store or a hardware store.

Gasoline: Gasoline is fairly cheap, and as long as you use a grade that is as pure as possible, you will find it an excellent vehicle. Lighter fuel is used by many artists with complete success. It is a technically sound practice to 'wash in' the first draft of an oil painting with colour diluted with gasoline, oilier vehicles being reserved for the final or top coats, according to the old craftsman's precept 'Begin lean and finish fat'.

Wax mixtures and *varnish mixtures:* These mixtures sometimes appeal to artists who wish to produce pictures with particularly smooth surfaces or extraordinarily thick 'impasto', but if you want to work without having to worry about the purely technical processes you should leave them alone until you have had a considerable amount of experience.

PALETTE CUPS   Small metal palette cups which cost only a few cents can be bought as containers for oil painting vehicles. Having a turned-over lip, they keep the liquid from spilling, and most have a springy metal clip on the underside by which they can be held on a palette. If you wish, you can use eggcups, tin lids or small pots instead, but these are more liable to be upset at inconvenient moments.

Ideally, you should have at least two containers by you when you are painting—one to hold your chosen vehicle; the other, a larger container, to hold some cheap gasoline, kerosene or turpentine substitute with which you can keep your brushes clean (a piece of cotton rag is useful for wiping them, incidentally). If colours are allowed to accumulate at the base of the bristles of a brush the fresh, unsullied mixtures that give so much pleasure in oil painting just cannot be obtained.

BRUSHES Brushes sold for oil painting can be roughly divided into two classes—soft brushes, made with sable or similar hair, and hard brushes, made from hoghair or bristle. You can manage quite successfully with hard brushes alone, but as soft brushes are not suitable for manipulating very stiff paint you cannot rely on sables, unaided.

Hoghair brushes are made in a number of different shapes, of which flat brushes and filbert brushes, shown in Illustration 28, are perhaps the most generally useful. They are marketed in sizes ranging from No. 1 (small) to No. 12 (very big). Choose medium size brushes—say, No. 7, No. 8 and No. 10— when you are starting, and look for brushes with bristles that will keep their resilience even when they are fully loaded with paint. You can usually test the quality of a brush by flicking its bristles sharply back with the end of your finger; or, if you are allowed to, dip them for a few seconds in cold water. If the bristles become flaccid when moistened, do not buy the brush.

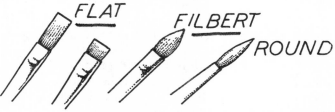

28. These are the brushes most often used for oil painting

Large sable brushes are useful for laying flat areas of colour with a minimum of unevenness, and small sable brushes are splendid for painting details exactly, but unfortunately they do not stand up to punishment as well as the tougher bristle brushes, and coarse grounds tend to wear them away.

All brushes should be washed out carefully with soap and warm water at the end of a day's work, and then rinsed thoroughly with clean water until all traces of paint and soap have disappeared. STORE UPRIGHT

A PALETTE   You can make a palette out of almost any rectangular piece of plywood of a suitable size. Cut a thumb hole out, as shown on the left of Illustration 29, chamfer the edges of the hole so that they will not bear hardly on your thumb, and rub several coats of linseed oil into the wood, leaving at least two days to elapse between each coat so that the oil will harden. If you do this carefully, an impermeable dully polished patina will result, and it will make a perfect surface for mixing colours on.

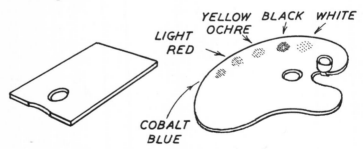

29. Two types of palette commonly used for oil painting

Although a rectangular palette will probably be easier to fit into a box or case when you are setting out on a sketching expedition, you may prefer to have a curved or 'studio' palette for indoor work. It will be important to get one of a suitable

78

shape if you do, for a badly balanced palette can cause fatigue and, even, discomfort. A well-designed palette that is sold commercially is shown on the right of Illustration 29, complete with a palette cup and a few compatible colours. You will notice that these are arranged near, but not immediately adjacent to, the outside edge of the palette. Specially reversed palettes can be supplied for left-handed people without extra charge—so, if you need one, don't hesitate to ask.

CANVASES AND OTHER SUPPORTS Ready-prepared canvases that are sold on tongued and grooved wooden stretchers are quite expensive, so you may prefer to make your earliest sketches in oils on one of the cheaper substitutes sold specially for students. There are oiled papers, for instance, and special painting boards. Wallboard and strawboard can be 'primed' with size to reduce their absorbency and then given a coat or two of white paint to conceal their undesirably raw colours.

Perhaps the most satisfactory support that is both cheap and strong is ordinary household hardboard. This has no great tendency to warp, as has plywood, and it will take paint on the smooth shiny side, or on the rough reverse, once a suitable 'ground' has been applied.

Laying a ground is a technical process that should not prove difficult as long as you understand fully the purpose of the ground. You will be trying to provide a suitable surface on which you can paint, and you will be doing it in such a way that you will have full control over its tone, colour and texture. All grounds consist of some opaque material, such as whiting (calcium carbonate) or white lead powder, which is held on the base or support by a suitable liquid, or mixture of liquids.

White lead paint makes a good ready-to-use ground, but it takes rather a long time to harden thoroughly, and it may have a tendency to turn yellow with time.

More inert grounds can be prepared by stirring whiting or

GESSO

79

fine slaked plaster of Paris into a solution of size or glue so that the mixture has the consistency of thin cream. If you are unable to obtain ready-slaked plaster, stir some fresh plaster in a bucket of water for half an hour or so, so that all its solidifying tendencies are over, then let it settle and pour all the water away.

Lay your grounds with a soft, flat brush, moving the brush in one direction only across the surface to be covered. When the first coat has dried out thoroughly, rub it down very gently with a sheet of fine glasspaper, and then add a second coat, and, later, perhaps a third and a fourth, moving the brush each time at right angles to the direction of the previous coat. A final coat of very thin size, applied when the ground is quite dry, will make it less absorbent.

Some artists do not like to have dazzling white grounds to paint on—they prefer to start with coloured or toned surfaces, and to superimpose white paint only where they decide to have the 'high lights' of their pictures. This would be a perfectly satisfactory procedure if oil colours were entirely inert, but unfortunately they tend to become slightly more transparent as the years pass, and an underlying tone or colour may darken perceptibly the picture that has been painted on top. Experiment with tinted or toned grounds if you like, but do so with your eye on the possible consequences.

EASELS   It is difficult to hold a canvas or panel on one's knee, as one can a drawing board or a sketchbook, so an easel is almost indispensable for oil painting. Ideally, you should have a heavy studio or radial easel, for working at home, and a light folding easel for outdoor sketching, but as you may well have to manage with one easel only you will be well advised to opt for the latter. Folding easels that are light, portable and rigid can be bought for five or ten dollars from any good artists' supplies dealer. Look for simplicity when you are buying a sketching easel. An easel that is all wing nuts and gadgets may not be nearly as useful as an easel you can erect in the twinkling of an eye.

DIRECT PAINTING   When you are learning to paint, you will probably want to achieve some results as directly as possible, without building up your paint surface laboriously in a series of undercoats and glazes by the strictly correct classical methods. If you have never done any oil painting before, you may appreciate this brief résumé of the first steps you can safely take when you are starting a landscape, a still life or a portrait.

(a) First, you should set out your colours near the edge of the palette in a convenient order. If you keep to this order consistently, your brush will travel to the correct destination almost automatically when you are painting with great urgency.

(b) Then you should sketch in the main forms of the picture with charcoal, or with a brush charged with a thin wash of some fairly neutral colour, such as blue-grey or raw umber. Gasoline or turpentine should be used for diluting the colour for this earliest 'lay-in'. If you use charcoal, you should dust off or fix with fixative all the surplus powder before you start to paint or it may make your colours seem very dull and dirty.

(c) Then, if you are pleased with the 'composition' you have tentatively arranged, you can mix up the colours you need for your painting and you can put them on the canvas in the places you have allotted to them, removing with a palette knife any colours that do not satisfy you or modifying them in any way you please by adding more colours, or by blending colours together. You will not make your picture any less permanent by superimposing one coat of paint over another, as long as the underlying coat is still wet, and has not formed a skin.

81

If the time you have available for painting runs out before you have finished your picture take a sheet of clean newspaper or some other absorbent paper, lay it over the paint surface, and rub gently with the flat of your hand on the outer side. The paper will then draw up all the surplus paint and vehicle and it will soften the outlines of the work, leaving a diffused image that will make a splendid foundation for work on the following day.

GLAZING The technically expert masters of the great ages of painting would probably have scorned the directness of the methods just described. They preferred to build up their paint surfaces slowly, allowing each coat to dry out thoroughly, sometimes over a period of many months, before adding the next. It is not very likely that you will want to adopt such a slow, deliberate technique in our hurried, worried century, but at least you should know what glazes are, so that you can produce, if any occasion demands it, the incomparable effects which result when a hard transparent or translucent film of colour is superimposed on a suitably ordered underpainting. The underpainting, in a classical masterpiece, would be carried out in tones of a single colour or 'monochrome'. Usually, some fairly neutral earth colour would be used, such as raw umber, yellow ochre, terre verte or burnt sienna. The purpose of the underpainting would be to develop the light and shade of the picture, without any reference to the local colours that would eventually be used.

Then, when the underpainting had had enough time to become bone hard right through, glazes would be prepared with which luminous, stained-glass-like colours could be superimposed. Transparent vehicles, mostly compounded from copal varnish and turpentine, would be used so that the glazes could be laid easily and fluently in place. Glazing was—and is— a process unfitted for bodgers and bunglers, but in the careful

82

hands of an expert it can produce some amazingly rich and colourful effects.

PAINTING WITH PALETTE KNIVES When you are choosing equipment for oil painting, you will probably be tempted to buy at least one palette knife—one of the easily cleaned and specially shaped knives with thin and fairly flexible blades that are used by artists for manipulating paints on the palette. If a palette knife is used, brushes can be spared the onus of general duties, which can only cause precious hairs or bristles to deteriorate. You may be tempted to buy a 'painting knife', too, which will be rather like a palette knife, but will probably have a more sharply tapered blade and a more pointed end.

One of the great advantages of palette knives and painting knives is their splendid versatility—they can be used for applying paint to a canvas or panel, as well as for mixing pigments and clearing away any surplus material at the end of a day. Obviously, pictures painted with palette knives will tend to demand more pigment—and, therefore, will be much more expensive to carry out—than pictures carried out exclusively with thin delicate washes of well-diluted colour. They may not be as permanent, either, for a thick crust of paint, unevenly distributed, will not be as inert after its outer surface has 'dried' as a thin coat of uniform depth. But pictures painted with palette knives have a vigour and richness that can only be simulated with the utmost difficulty in pictures painted by more traditional means. There are few paint surfaces more exciting than those to be encountered in the works of one of the foremost exponents of palette knife painting, such as R. O. Dunlop. One can get almost as much sensuous enjoyment from the sight of fat encrustations of pigment on a canvas as one can from a close inspection of jewels, or precious fabrics, or matchless silver.

83

VARNISHING When you have finished an oil painting, you may wish to give it a coat of varnish to protect its surface from the harmful vapours, gases and dirt that abound in the atmosphere, especially in and near cities, to bring out its colours, or to give its surface a uniformly shiny, semi-shiny or matt finish. If you decide to take the chance—and varnishing is quite a risky business, since a coat which becomes dirty or discoloured cannot be easily removed—you should wait at least a year, to let all the underlying layers of paint dry out thoroughly, before you venture.

Then, you should choose the right varnish to suit the particular circumstances. Copal varnish, made by dissolving hard resins in linseed (or a similar) oil, is one of the most permanent varnishes you can buy, but if anything goes wrong you will find it almost impossible to remove. Mastic varnish, made by dissolving softer resins in volatile spirit, can be removed comparatively easily with benzine or some similar solvent, but there is no guarantee that the underlying painting will not be damaged in the process. In spite of their drawbacks, these two, the best-known varnishes, are almost certainly the best for the amateur painter to use.

Varnishing should always be carried out on a warm sunny day, when the humidity is low. If you must clean the painting let it dry thoroughly before you apply the varnish, or an ugly mist or 'bloom' may develop under the surface. Then, when all is ready, and there is no danger of dust or dirt intruding, lay the painting flat on its back on a steady table or working surface and apply the varnish with a large flat soft brush. The varnish may take a day or more to dry, so you will have to devise some sort of cover to keep impurities from settling on it during this time.

84

NINE

COMPOSITION

When you are sketching from nature, and trying to record the outward appearance of a building, a stretch of country or a group of figures or animals, you will not have much chance to worry about the placing of your drawing or painting on the paper or canvas you are using. When you are starting to build up a picture that is to be as complete and satisfying a work of art as you can create you will be engaged on a conscious and deliberate piece of planning from the very first mark you make. That's the difference between a 'study' and a 'composition'. When you are making a study, your eyes will be fixed firmly on the world before you, except for occasional glances at your work. When you are engaged on a composition, at least half your attention will be turned to the processes of selection, simplification and arrangement. The two attitudes are quite compatible—it's just a matter of which is in the ascendancy at any particular time.

Not all the great pictures that are hanging on the walls of world-famous art galleries are completely satisfying compositions. Far from it. Many of them were painted by men who were too busy extending the frontiers of our visual knowledge to have much time or mental energy left for purely pictorial problems such as those of balance or tonal pattern-making. Monet, for instance, was so intent on capturing the sun-lit radiance of a garden in summer that he painted some excellent canvases without using any really dark tones at all. Uccello, further back in history, arranged the dead warriors and their weapons in one of his most famous battle scenes in neat, parallel rows because he was engrossed, at the time he painted it, in the study of linear perspective. But, in spite of these exceptions, there is no better way of learning how to compose a picture satisfactorily than by studying the works of the great masters. An afternoon spent constructively in any art museum of one of our larger cities will teach you more than any number of textbooks.

BALANCE One of the first problems to be solved by an artist who is deliberately composing a picture is that posed by the necessity to make the picture 'balance'—that is, to look as if its component parts are completely static and could not have been better ordered. To help you to understand what is meant by this, let us consider the quality of symmetry which underlies so much fine design. You will almost certainly know what a symmetrical shape or pattern is like—the ink blot shown on the left of Illustration 30 is a symmetrical one, because it has been produced by folding a piece of paper in two, and squeezing out ink quite equally on to both sides of the centre line. The blot shown on the right of the illustration is asymmetrical —that is to say, it cannot be divided into two identical halves, and it could be said to lack 'balance'.

30. Two ink blots—one symmetrical (left)
and one asymmetrical

Let us see how conscious great artists can be of symmetry when they are planning their pictures. Illustration 31 shows a simple linear analysis of the famous painting 'The Avenue at Middelharnis', by Hobbema. So small a sketch can only act as a reminder, it cannot convey any of the great breadth and dignity of this magnificent landscape, but it can show you how Hobbema used the basic symmetry of the scene to produce the serene, settled atmosphere of a peaceful country lane. There are minor differences between the trees, hedges and buildings to the right and to the left of the road, but these differences are too subtle to affect the pronounced and beautifully controlled regularity of the major plan.

31. The composition of this famous painting by Hobbema is nearly symmetrical

Illustration 32 shows a similarly simplified analysis of the Visitation, by Mariotto Albertinelli, who died in A.D. 1515. Here, the original symmetry of the composition is stressed by the central view of the framing arch, but the two figures, one on each side of the centre line of the picture, are most sensitively contrasted, while not being made so different that the basic unity of the composition is destroyed. If you ever get a chance to study this great painting at close quarters, or in a really good reproduction, notice how Albertinelli has used the dark sleeve and drapery of the light figure on the right to balance the light face, hands and skirt that he has used to make less heavy the dark figure on the left. Tonally, this design is inspired, and to many people is as satisfying as any of the works of Albertinelli's more celebrated contemporary, Raphael.

32. A simplified analysis of the Visitation by Albertinelli

Once your sense of balance has been developed by study and experiment you should be able to create some completely satisfactory compositions that have no basis in symmetry at all. You will develop an awareness of tonal pattern, on which all success in pictorial composition ultimately depends, if in every great painting you see you look out for the large unvaried areas of dark, light or intermediate tone known, usually, to artists as 'masses'. You should look out for these simple broad shapes in every landscape and interior that catches your attention, too. When you can resolve a complex mass of buildings or a leafy clump of trees into one simple shape, all of a single tone, with a silhouette that is not only recognisable but accurate you will be well on the way to being able to achieve the same beautiful simplicity in your work as Whistler, Peter de Wint and the other great masters who learned to disregard all inessential details almost as soon as they could draw. Whistler acquired his love of simplicity by studying the perfect tonal organisation of imported Japanese prints. Have you ever studied the compositions of Utamaro, say, and Hokusai? If you haven't, your own work will almost certainly improve out of all recognition when you do.

A good example of simplification can be seen in John Sell Cotman's view of Greta Bridge, in Yorkshire, which is reproduced in Plate 2.

RECTANGULAR COMPOSITIONS Pictures that are drawn or painted in rectangular shapes—which includes most sheets of paper and most canvases—can be given strength, balance and an appearance of being properly integrated if a certain number of vertical and horizontal lines are cunningly concealed in their basic structure. These lines need not be exactly parallel to the sides of the paper or canvas, and it is not a good thing to have too many of them, but they are extremely valuable from a purely pictorial point of view. A picture that is based entirely on diagonals and near-diagonals may give a striking impression of restless activity, but it will never give the viewer the feeling of classical serenity that can be conveyed by a picture based on a straight up, straight down and straight across scaffolding.

Does the idea of including specially contrived lines and rhythms in your pictures disturb you? If you don't see how it can be done without obtruding the mechanics of picture-making on the attention of the viewer, look at Illustration 33, which shows a linear analysis of Jan Vermeer's lovely 'Young

Lady at the Virginals'. The vertical and horizontal lines in this composition would not be noticed by many untrained observers, whose eyes would rest primarily on the central figure, but how essential they are in creating the atmosphere of monumental simplicity that is the hallmark of nearly all Vermeer's work!

Of course, there is one horizontal line that will be present in

33. The composition of Vermeer's 'Young Lady at the Virginals' is founded firmly on vertical and horizontal lines

almost every picture, even if it is hidden and appreciated only by the subconscious mind, and that is the horizon itself. As soon as you start to draw or paint any landscape or interior you will have to make up your mind about its position on your paper or canvas. Will it be near the lowest edge, so that your picture is nearly all sky? Will it be near the upper edge, so that your picture is nearly all floor or ground? The only place on which it should not be allowed to fall without a lot of careful consideration is bang across the centre of the rectangle, because

90

there it will be liable to split the picture exactly in half, breaking it down into two equal and conflicting divisions, each of which will make its own disturbing claim on the spectator's attention. Similarly, a particularly bold upright line—as, for example, that made by a poplar or similar tree, by a church steeple, or by a tall standing figure—should be placed either slightly to the right or slightly to the left of the middle of the picture, and never on the dangerous centre point, where it may do its destructive cleaving.

Once you have become accustomed to the uses (and abuses) of vertical and horizontal lines you may feel inclined to start your picture-planning by sketching a few faint lines across a tentative rectangle. On such a vague exploratory basis many of the world's greatest masterpieces have been created, the discipline imposed by a pre-ordained arrangement of satisfying shapes being sufficient to bring the worst excesses of the most romantic imagination under control.

THE ANATOMY OF A PICTURE   We have just been considering the enormous importance of the centre lines of a picture, but there are other parts of a rectangular pictorial composition that have to be organised carefully if the arrangement is not to look sad and contrived.

The corners, for example.   WHERE DOES IT GO?

If the eye of the viewer is not to be led vainly away towards the frame by the converging sides of the picture, some sort of a device must be found to steer the gaze unobtrusively round and towards the central components of the picture again. Clouds can be used, in the sky part of a picture, and shadows on the ground if no more substantial features are already suggested by the actual subject. Constable and his contemporaries were adept at introducing bushes, rocks, brambles, ferns and other small ingredients of the countryside into their pictures in such a way that the compositions became so perfect

that their very excellence does not attract attention—we take it for granted! But the bushes, rocks, brambles or ferns may not have been in the spots represented when the artists arrived to paint their chosen scenes. Faced with a blank, uninteresting foreground an artist may have to borrow as many features as he needs from neighbouring landscapes, or even from sketches he has made elsewhere on previous occasions. Nature may have to be manipulated slightly if full use is to be made of its pictorial possibilities. The artist is not, after all, just a human camera. The beauty of nature and the beauty of art are two quite different things.

And this pictorial sleight of hand may be needed to produce a sufficiently compelling centre of interest, too. Most painters find that the artistic value of their pictures is increased if one focal point in the composition is emphasised at the expense of all others. A group of figures in the foreground of a landscape may be given a little extra value, for example, by colour, by tone or by sheer good drawing so that the eye is brought back to them almost compulsively every time it has been attracted into the further recesses of the picture. If no group of figures, or other feature, is sufficiently interesting to be accented in this way, it is quite legitimate to introduce one. There is no need to be quite as ingenuous as the Victorian amateur painters who used cows almost automatically when blank foregrounds proved too much for their powers of invention. Look at John Crome's famous 'Poringland Oak' if you get a chance, and see how much his study of that great tree owes to the bathing figures in the foreground. If those figures had not been there when Crome painted his original study, he would almost certainly have had to invent them. They are, ultimately, indispensable.

92

[Handwritten margin notes: EYES; FOCAL POINT; DELIBERATE; SMALL AIRPLANE + EYES / SEARCH "JOURNEY"; CREATES "THE SEARCH" FOR THE SMALL AIRPLANE IN THE PAINTING - (IN THE SKY / CLOUDS)]

TEN

PAINTING A PORTRAIT

Look at any one of the great portraits by Rembrandt in a large art museum and you will know, if you have any sensibility at all, that you are in the presence of one of the world's most valuable masterpieces—valuable artistically, that is to say, as well as virtually priceless materially. The portrait of Margaretha Trip is the profoundest possible statement about a proud and infinitely experienced old person, the portrait of the Jewish merchant is as much of an enigma as the better known Mona Lisa by Leonardo, while the portraits of Rembrandt himself done in maturity are among the most moving human documents it would be possible to imagine. Yet each of these portraits contains only one single figure—and only part of one at that—seen as if in the ray of a spotlight against a slightly monotonous dark background. What is the quality that makes them so precious and unique, when portraits of sitters who were—and are—much more beautiful and appealing stare at us in reproduction from the covers of a great many of the glossy journals we pick up?

To attempt to answer that question we shall have to look closely at a poor, commercially produced portrait, to see where it falls down.

First, we shall probably see that the figure is badly placed on the canvas—it is either too high, or too low, or too much to one side. The placing of Rembrandt's figures is usually superb. Look at the pattern made by the dark and light shapes in the portrait of Margaretha Trip, for instance. Rembrandt has placed her head slightly to the right of the centre line, you will notice, so that there is rather more background on the side she is facing than behind her head (this is a very safe principle to follow, until you are able to place a figure

93

ırreproachably, almost by instinct). When you are starting to draw or paint a portrait, you should make a few trial layouts first on a piece of spare paper, so that you will not have to waste time on vain experiments when you are working on the version that you hope will be the final one.

Next, we shall probably see that the figure is badly drawn—the features may all be delineated with the utmost care but somehow they do not fit together to make a really convincing face. Rembrandt was a splendid draughtsman—possibly one of the greatest the world has ever known. It is the combination in his work of breadth of vision and meticulous attention to detail that makes his portraits so exciting to examine, both at long range and at extremely close quarters.

Finally, we shall probably see that the colours in the commercial portrait lack the lovely unity that gives the bronze and golden shades of the Rembrandt their incomparable charm. Rembrandt used a restricted palette, but with a few colours he created the most delightful harmonies, which cannot be matched by better equipped painters who have not developed his sensibility. A crudely coloured portrait may catch the attention, but it is not likely to hold it for very long.

But, you may be saying, all this is very obvious—we all know that no present-day commercial painter is likely to have the same designing ability, power of draughtsmanship and colour sense of an old master. What has this got to do with *my* first attempts to paint a recognisable portrait?

The answer is, a lot. Each of the ways in which Rembrandt's portraits are so vastly superior can tell you something about your own approach and teach you how to set about your task in a sensible step by step fashion, making sure that each of your preparations and procedures is sound and technically correct before you go on to the next.

Here, then, are a few notes which may show you how you can most profitably take your earliest steps in portrait painting.

GOOD AND BAD SITTERS There are two kinds of sitter that you will have to learn to discriminate between—people whose physical make-up lends itself to good portraiture, and those whose physical make-up just doesn't. Learning that is even more vital than learning to discriminate between people who can sit still and those who can't, and that is important enough.

A professional portrait painter is not able to turn the bad sitters away, unless he is enormously successful and can afford to choose which commissions he accepts and which he tactfully declines. Some of our annual exhibitions of paintings, which are little more than trade shows, are most depressingly burdened with portraits that have been ordered for prestige reasons, or for personal pride, and are not real works of art at all. They show over-fed, over-decorated and not over-handsome or beautiful citizens, with whom the painters have clearly been barely in sympathy, and whose features might well have been more suitably and economically recorded by being put in front of a camera.

In that respect, you will be more fortunate. You will be able to ask any of your relations or friends to pose for you, looking primarily for a sitter with a face that can be subdivided into good clear-cut planes—a round, puppy-fat face can be most attractive, but it may be very difficult to draw. You should look, too, for that strange intangible quality known to most of us as 'character'. You may not be able to express a man's greed, happiness, irritability, fortitude or any other facets of his character by the way you paint his face, but the sum total of all his traits will affect his personal appearance, and if his character is interesting he will make a much better subject for your pen or brush than someone whose personality is, literally, 'colourless'.

Then, when you have selected your model, you should decide how he, or she, should sit.

In art schools and colleges, and in some painters' studios, models are usually placed on a low platform or throne, so that a seated figure will be nearer the eye level of the artist, and a standing figure will be partly above it. This is not essential, though, and you and your sitter will probably be happier with a less formal arrangement. As a support and surroundings for a figure it is difficult to improve on an ordinary chair in an ordinary room, among the everyday furnishings the artist is used to, and knows. Don't put your sitter in a contorted or unnatural pose, or ask for any expression but one that is serenely relaxed. A smiling face may be one of the most attractive sights in the world—'I wish I could capture that fleeting smile', how often we hear that said—but to ask someone to hold a smile through a painting session an hour or two long is not only unkind, it will also probably introduce an unwanted element of caricature into your work.

Sitting still while someone else makes a painting of you can be an extremely tedious and boring occupation, especially for people who have a normal amount of nervous energy. You can make things a bit more interesting for your sitters by putting books or newspapers near enough for them to read, or, alternatively, you can set all poses in such a way that your sitters can look out of a window or an open doorway into a garden, a street or some other place where a certain amount of visual activity may help to while away the time.

Don't keep anyone standing or sitting for more than a quarter of an hour or twenty minutes without asking if he or she would like a rest. Most professional models can remain motionless for nearly an hour, but a lot of experience is required before any conscious human being can remain inert for so long, so don't turn a painting session into an endurance test. Before a rest begins, you can outline with chalk on the supporting surfaces the positions of your sitter's feet, hands, thighs and any other convenient portions of the anatomy, then it will be possible for the pose to be resumed without any difficulty or bewilderment at the end of the recess.

ARRANGING THE PICTURE Before you start work, make sure that your sitter is posed under the best possible conditions. If light is falling on to a figure from several different directions —as, for example, from three widely spaced windows—it may be rather difficult for you to represent the main forms on a two-dimensional surface, using the interplay of light and dark described in Chapter Four. To make your task easier, at least until you have had a certain amount of experience, try to arrange for a single source of light to illuminate your sitter, and if possible let this be to one side of the subject—a light falling from behind the artist will tend to flatten all forms; a light shining in his eyes will tend to dazzle him and turn all intervening shapes into dark silhouettes with narrow light edges. A subtle glow of light can be introduced into the shadowy sides of forms, if they are too murky, by large sheets of white paper placed unobtrusively to act as reflectors.

When you are sure that your lighting is as informative as you can make it, check that the background of your figure will enhance your picture and not obtrude itself on the attention in any unpleasant or disturbing way. If you are in doubt about this, don't hesitate to look for a large piece of drapery that you can hang up behind the sitter to provide a pleasant but fairly neutral screen. Often, a sheet, blanket or curtain suspended by one corner or edge will arrange itself in such simple and monumental folds that it makes a perfect foil to the intricate complexities of a closely observed figure—a fact fully realised by the great court portrait painters of the seventeenth and eighteenth centuries, who rarely failed to introduce a few yards of subtly patterned silk brocade or some other attractively rich material into the sumptuous surroundings they were paid to reproduce.

Then, make a few quick sketches of your sitter. When you are doing this, you should not only be deciding how to arrange on your paper or canvas the forms you can actually see, as suggested a little earlier in this chapter, but you should also be prepared to change the pose slightly or to readjust any part of the background if by doing so you can make the arrangement of your picture more agreeable. You may decide to fasten one corner of the background drapery a little higher, for instance, so that the folds hang in some particular way that you think will help the composition; you may decide that the tone or colour of part of the background needs altering; you may even ask your sitter to change some article of dress, or an accessory, that does not sit happily in your general plan. By the time you have finished, and are really satisfied with both sitter and background, you will be ready to start away on the portrait proper. It will seem all the easier for you to carry out if the scene in front of you is completely to your liking, in every respect.

SIMPLICITY AND STRUCTURE) In your first tentative lay-in of a figure drawing or painting you will concentrate, if you are wise, on establishing the main planes of the body, limbs and head in the simplest possible way. Don't try to draw round the outlines, or get involved in any exact delineation of details, but force yourself to think of every part of your sitter as a solid form which has a front, back and sides, and, maybe, a top and a bottom as well.

The drawing on the left of Illustration 34 shows how a head can be blocked in lightly, with each of the main planes established according to a simple lighting scheme—the planes on one side, facing the left of the illustration, are as light as they can be; the planes on the other side, facing the right of the illustration, are dark; and the front-facing planes, which do not receive full illumination, are allotted a half-tone, or medium shade of grey. This may seem a crude and arbitrary way of building up a form as subtle and as full of gentle nuances of surface as a human head, but it gives the artist the best possible chance of assessing the correct proportions of each part, and

98

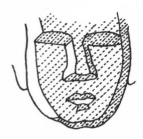
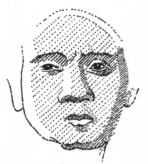

34. This shows how the main planes of a head can be established before any attempt is made to render details

of assembling all the parts in their correct relationship to the whole.

After you have checked and re-checked the shape of all the parts of a head that has been simplified in this way (or of any other complex form, for that matter) you can make the dividing lines or 'arrises' between the main planes a little less obvious, and you can start to look for, and include, some of the minor changes of plane mentioned earlier. Bear in mind—if you are using colour—the contrasting qualities of warm and cool colours described in Chapter Five, and decide at as early a stage as possible whether the light that is playing on your sitter is predominantly warm or predominantly cool. If you can't decide, plump for one or other, derive all the shadows from the opposite side of the colour circle, and don't deviate from your scheme or you will destroy the precious feeling of simplicity and unity you should be striving so hard to retain.

Are you worried about catching the likeness of a sitter, which so many people think is the be-all and end-all of portraiture? If you are, you will find that you are much more likely to produce a recognisable representation of your model if you build your drawing or painting up in simplified, structural facets, very much as if you are carving it out of Plasteline or some other fairly soft material with bold movements of a carving knife. Any attempts you make to produce a pair of appealing, arresting or just plain beautiful eyes on your paper or canvas will be efforts made in vain unless those eyes are firmly embedded in a head that is structurally sound.

HANDS Hands may play almost as important a part in a drawn or painted portrait as the head, since clumsily delineated extremities force themselves on the attention and distract the viewer from the artist's chosen centre of interest. Illustration 35 shows how a hand can be blocked in in a simple, logical way.

35. A complex part of the body, such as the hand,
can be most easily drawn if it is studied in easy stages

First, the practically rigid, virtually flat mass known as the palm is studied—it is given this priority because the fingers and thumbs can only be located accurately once a proper foundation for them has been established.

Then lines are drawn that indicate the general direction and length of each of the digits. Most people underestimate the size of a sitter's hands (try putting your own right hand over your face, if you have no idea of the relative extent of these two areas of the body) and not many people stress the firm, bony quality of the fingers until they have had a great deal of experience. The drawing on the right of Illustration 35 may seem a bit hard and mechanical, but if you can make a structural study like that you will be erring on the right side. Too many people who are learning to draw produce studies of hands that look more like soft, flabby bunches of bananas.

ELEVEN

PAINTING A LANDSCAPE

Although you may never feel the urge to paint a portrait—
many people do not care for the possible embarrassments of a
close, sustained scrutiny of somebody else's features—you will
almost certainly want to paint landscapes almost as soon as
you have equipped yourself with paints and brushes and know
how to handle them. The word 'landscape' is not only used to
describe paintings of pastoral country scenes, incidentally.
It is used by many artists to cover all outdoor views, whether
in towns, near rivers, amid mountains or by the sea, as well as
on open farmland. And that is the sense in which it will be
used in this chapter. You won't want to spend all your painting
time within the four walls of your home, even if you live in the
heart of a crowded city.

Before we examine the preparations that may be necessary
when you intend to set out on an outdoor sketching expedition,
it may be valuable to give a little thought to the revolutionary
change in attitude to landscape painting that was initiated by
the great English artist John Constable in the first half of the
nineteenth century. Before that time it was thought quite
proper for artists to compose their outdoor pictures in the
comparatively comfortable surroundings of their studios.
Gainsborough, it is recorded, built up little model landscapes
at home out of stones, sticks and moss, and then made studies
of them, using these sketches as the bases on which to construct
his larger pictures. Other artists, less conscientious and enter-
prising than Gainsborough, did not even bother to make
models, relying on certain formulas for picture-making that
had been handed down from master to pupil for several genera-
tions. Constable had no patience with artistic clichés of any

101

kind. He wanted to study nature direct, trusting only the evidence of his own eyesight. His great studies of Salisbury, Suffolk and Hampstead Heath, painted in the open air, had the same kind of explosive effect on his fellow-artists as the first exhibitions of several ultra-progressive art movements have had in the twentieth century. The shock value of his use of fresh natural greens and the impact of his brilliant observation of the effects of sunlight made the public dissatisfied with the brown tones and predictable compositions of many of his contemporaries, and his work paved the way for the infinitely varied researches carried on a little later by the members of the Barbizon School, the French Impressionists and other groups who were committed to painting 'on the spot', and not at second or third hand.

When you decide, like Constable and those who followed him, to work in the open air you will find it difficult to do without a folding easel, to hold your drawing board or canvas, and a box or case of some kind in which to carry your paints and other materials—unless, that is, you are going to use water colours exclusively, or unless you are going to be content with comparatively small sketches made in a book that can be held in the hand.

Excellent sketching bags, made from superior quality canvas, and fitted with adjustable shoulder straps, outside pockets with gussets, and straps to hold a stool and an easel can be obtained for five or ten dollars.

More expensive, but extremely useful, are the polished hardwood sketching units marketed by several well-known manufacturers of artists' equipment. Each of these units combines a complete oil colour box, a painting table with adjustable legs, and an easel, which pack away together to form a neat portable box that is not much larger than the average man's brief-case.

If you are unable to afford such a case ready made, you can adapt almost any suitable container by using a little ingenuity, adding clips, straps and compartments to keep the various items of equipment apart while you are on your travels.

Among the other accessories you may find useful when you are out sketching are:

A sunhat, preferably one that will keep the glare out of your eyes, as well as off the back of your neck.

Insecticide, that will ward off flies and other pests.

A sandwich tin and a flask, for light refreshments.

Some Bulldog clips. These are most useful on windy days for holding sheets of paper that might otherwise be blown away.

Rags, for cleaning brushes, and mopping up.

Canvas pins, with double steel points, by which wet oil paintings can be carried home in pairs, face to face, without damage.

CHOOSING A SUBJECT A book written nearly fifty years ago, and still on the shelves of most public libraries, divides Great Britain into areas which are suitable for landscape painting in water colours, and those which are not. Further, it lists the landmarks in each area that are picturesque enough to be worth painting—even prescribing the exact spots from which the artist should view most of them when he is planning his pictures.

In the years that have elapsed since that book was written, the idea that only certain old and romantic places can commend themselves to a painter has gone right out of fashion. Artists of considerable stature have found pictorially rewarding subjects in the most unlikely places—L. S. Lowry, for example, has shown us that even the back streets of grim industrial Lancashire towns have a most potent beauty all of their own, and Graham Sutherland enlarged his reputation considerably by finding new and highly significant subjects in the shabby wreckage of bombed London houses.

103

The whole world, then, is yours to explore, and to comb for possible themes. The only limitations that may affect you are purely practical ones. Perhaps you should memorise a few of the possible snags before you set out. You may be too eager to start work to think about them once you have spotted a subject that really interests you.

The sun: Don't set up your easel, even in cloudy weather, without considering carefully the position of the sun, and even more important is its probable position in a few hours' time. With the sun directly behind you, the landscape before you will seem extremely colourful, but the forms will tend to seem rather flat, and their cast shadows will tend to converge towards a Vanishing Point on the horizon. With the sun shining from one side, the distribution of light and shade will be well adjusted, and the forms will still be reasonably colourful. With the sun shining in your eyes, you will probably find it very difficult to paint at all. The forms between you and the sun will be flattened, so that they look like dark cut-outs with dazzling edges, and their cast shadows, being nearer to you than the forms themselves, will seem disproportionately important. It may not be easy for you to be sun- and shadow-conscious during a dull patch on a showery day, but it will pay you to make the effort, because sunshine can seem especially powerful when there are clouds about, and when there is a lot of moisture in the atmosphere.

The wind: The wind that howls over the heath may be an effective ingredient in romantic poetry, but it can be an absolutely damnable deterrent even to the most determined painter. If you can't find a sheltered spot, drive the legs of your easel securely into the ground and tie some heavy boulders to them before you start work. It is disconcerting—to say the least of it—to find the picture you are trying to paint coming towards you suddenly in the teeth of a Force Nine gust. Oil colours can seem supernaturally sticky under such circumstances.

Landowners: Most farmers and other landowners will be kind enough to give you permission to paint on their ground as long as you are polite enough to ask for it first. The main exceptions to this rule are the people who have already suffered at the hands of discourteous intruders, but that is a risk one has to take. A little sincere admiration of a man's property will usually work wonders.

Animals: Curious cows, belligerent bulls and deafening dogs are normal hazards of the countryside, but their attentions can usually be avoided if a little foresight is brought to bear on the problem before it has had a chance to develop.

Other factors, such as freedom from children and other spectators, freedom from noise, and convenience of transportation, may have to be borne in mind, but no minor considerations are likely to stand in your way once you have found a subject that you know you really must paint, whatever the odds.

PROCEDURE Having established yourself in your chosen spot—and having set up your easel, if you are going to paint in oils—you should start work as quickly as you conveniently can. Hours will slip past and light will fade with astonishing rapidity once your attention is gripped by the problems in hand.

The exact procedure you will follow when you are starting the picture will be affected, of course, by the medium you are using, and the notes given already in the chapters on water colour painting and oil painting can be referred to. There are a few technical processes, though, that are common to all frequently used media, and here are some notes that may help you to remember them:

Breaking the white: Making the first marks on a spotless piece of paper or canvas can be an anxious business, but you will soon find your picture taking shape if you start to sketch very lightly with a fine piece of charcoal, rubbing away all the surplus carbon as you work with a clean piece of rag. Alternatively,

105

you can use a faint wash of brown, grey or blue, or even —when you have had a bit of experience—some diluted tints of the local colours you intend ultimately to use.

SKY

Painting a sky: Once you are satisfied with your original faint, tentative lay-in, you can start to apply the final coats of paint to your picture. There is no real reason why you should start to do this by painting the sky, but as you will have to put the first patch of full colour somewhere, so that you can relate all the other colours to it, it seems quite sensible to begin near the top of the paper or canvas, and to work downwards.

The sky is not like a flat blue wall, as strong in colour near the horizon as at the empyrean. Rather, you should think of it as Constable did, as an immense blue mixing bowl that has **DARK** been inverted over another huge inverting mixing bowl, which is the earth. Considered in this way, the gentle gradation of colour and tone from the rich blue above us to the pale, opalescent tints in the furthest distance seems perfectly logical.

LT

As you work downwards towards the horizon, be prepared to introduce any cloud forms that will help the composition of your picture, stressing the solidity of each form by recording the light and shade on it as exactly as you can. Remember that one part of a cloud may well be very much lighter than the sky behind it, while other parts of the same cloud may be very much darker than the adjoining blue. There is no easy way to paint clouds convincingly—all the greatest landscape painters have made innumerable studies of typical cloud formations, so that no impossible or even unlikely effects should be included in their work.

Near the horizon, any clouds that are still visible will almost certainly appear to be comparatively small, and to have a relatively limited amount of light and shade. When you are painting this part of a picture—the zone immediately above the 'skyline'—be prepared to lay in the faint, pale shapes of any mountains, distant buildings, or other far away features you may wish to include, before the 'air tint' has had a chance to dry. No part of a landscape that is more than a few hundred yards away from the artist will be sharply defined—distance lends mystery to the prospect before us, as well as enchantment.

Painting distant features: You can create a notable amount of 'atmosphere' in a landscape painting by using only the palest tones and the most subtle tints, with the greatest care, when you are delineating distant features. If you paint one shadow too dark or one colour too strong you may destroy in your picture the very spaciousness that impresses you in the real-life landscape before you.

Painting buildings: The appearance of all buildings in a realistic landscape will be conditioned to a certain extent by the principles of linear perspective reviewed briefly in Chapter Six. If you have an actual building before you—in the middle distance of a landscape, say—the task of assessing the angles of each part, and of discovering the relevant Vanishing Points, will be comparatively easy. Don't try to draw or paint any of the architectural details such as doors, windows, buttresses or mouldings until you are sure that you have established the main shape of the building correctly, with all the proportions of all its visible sides judged exactly, and their relationship to each other checked and re-checked. Details come *afterwards.*

The further a building is away from you, the fewer details you will see. Don't make the mistake of drawing or painting every window pane in a house a mile or so away from you. Keep all feats of architectural draughtsmanship for the foreground of a picture or they may destroy the whole scheme of logical recession on which the success of your pictorial composition, if it is an objective one, ultimately depends.

And while we are on the subject of buildings, don't be tempted into slack draughtsmanship by the superficial charms of crumbling cottages, jettied inns, beamed farms, derelict windmills, obsolete watermills and other reminders of more erratic and less hygienic ages than our own. Include picturesque buildings in your paintings if you like, but when you do so make sure that the structure of each building is sound—in your picture, at least—before you bend your attention and skill to the thick veil of ivy, wisteria or Virginia creeper with which it will almost certainly be shrouded. The textures of brickwork and stonework can be dangerously distracting, too—most amateur painters will spend hours minutely delineating the mortar lines between the bricks of a wall without considering either the tone value or the colour value of the wall when seen as a whole. The results of such misplaced conscientiousness are usually disastrous. Paint the whole wall first, before *sky* you think of it as the sum of a number of parts.

Painting trees: If you can draw trees successfully—and that, as was said in Chapter Six, is largely a matter of being able to analyse their characteristic forms of growth—you will be well on the way to being able to paint them successfully. With a brush in your hand, though, you will be better equipped to reproduce the full rhythms of summer foliage than when you are armed with a pencil alone. Study closely any tree you are trying to paint, and the smaller branches and leaves will seem to be arranged according to certain pre-ordained natural growth rhythms. Van Gogh used these rhythms with extraordinary success, building up thick encrustations of pigment on his canvases as he forced his paints to follow the vital, twisting forms of the cypress trees that moved him so intensely. Earlier painters, who planned their landscapes in their studios, would each evolve some kind of formula by which they could design a tree or a shrub to fill any undesirable gap in a composition. Look at some eighteenth-century 'fried parsley', as Blake called this made-to-order vegetation, and then look at Van Gogh's trees and the comparison will show you the difference between merely decorative work, and work that is the expression of some deeply felt emotion.

108

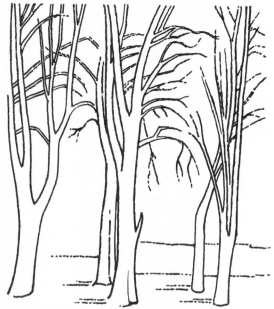

36. A profound study of the way trees grow gives strength to Cézanne's monumental landscapes. This is a simplified linear analysis of part of one of his most famous paintings

37. Compare this illustration with the analysis of Cézanne's tree forms in Illustration 36. Here Van Gogh is planning how to place his small blocks of heavily loaded pigment so that they will best express the vital, flame-like quality of a cypress tree

CLOUDS/ MADE UP OF WATER.

PAINT NOW, LEARN LATER

Painting water: A large proportion of the landscape subjects that attract you will contain a river, a lake, a pond or some other sheet of water, and this, being a reflecting surface, may easily disconcert you. Reflections are not unduly difficult to draw, though. You can delineate them as nearly as possible as you see them, if you are painting out of doors. If you are making up or completing a landscape at home you can refer to the little diagram on the left of Illustration 38, which shows why

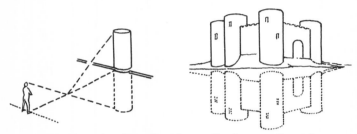

38. These drawings show how reflections are formed 'in' water and similar mirror-like surfaces

the reflected image of any point will appear to be immediately beneath that point, and as far below the surface of the water as the original point is above it. Once you have grasped the significance of that diagram, and have made a few rough sketches, perhaps, to see how the principle works out in practice, you will almost certainly find yourself attracted to painting sites that promise the suggestion of order and symmetry peculiar to waterside subjects. Some painters, notably Canaletto, Guardi, Turner, Claude Monet and Alfred Sisley, produced their finest and most memorable works by rivers or lagoons.

Painting a foreground: You should give a lot of thought to the placing of any people, animals, natural forms or inanimate objects you may decide to put in the foreground of a landscape,

110

as a prominent feature that is carelessly positioned may wreck a pictorial design that without it would be extremely pleasant.

Be especially careful about figures near the picture plane (that is, the imaginary 'sheet of glass' that divides the spectator from the contents of a picture frame). If the legs and feet of a figure in the foreground are out of sight, so that only a head and truncated torso are in the picture, the attention of all spectators will immediately be drawn, even if only subconsciously, to the hidden continuation of the ground plane, and this may be slightly worrying. The part of the world you have enclosed within the sides of a picture frame should seem to be a complete world in itself, even though, of course, it can never really be more than a fragment.

FINISHING A LANDSCAPE PAINTING 'A picture should be a more or less complete statement at each and every point in its development.' If that piece of wisdom is correct—and one hears it repeated often enough—there should be no such thing as a really unfinished landscape painting, but every artist knows how annoyed he feels when the light changes or the hour advances so much that further work is impossible.

There is a lot to be said for working only in short spells when one is painting out of doors. Shadows move and colour values alter most disconcertingly as the sun appears to cross the sky. Monet, the great French Impressionist, would take several canvases with him when he went out landscape painting, and he would work on each for about half an hour, discarding it as soon as there was any perceptible difference in the scene he was trying to portray. You may not be as fastidious as that, but you should be careful not to waste precious time and materials on a painting when all the original inspiration has gone. Some of the most profound statements made about the English countryside by the late Philip Wilson Steer are little more than vaporous colour notes dashed off in the heat of a moment.

111

TWELVE

THE SECRET WORLD

So far, this book has dealt almost exclusively with the equipment and materials necessary for drawing and painting, and with some of the elementary technical processes involved in objective art—that is, work in which the main emphasis is on the pictorial qualities of the visible world with all its oddities and its unpredictable charms. But realistic and figurative work is not the only kind that may interest you once you are fully equipped and have had a little experience. You may find that subjects drawn from the secret world of the imagination appeal much more to the romantic side of your nature. No two artists are alike—it will be up to you to explore all the possible fields of activity before you concentrate too rigidly on any one.

ABSTRACT ART You should try some exercises in abstraction, for instance.

Abstract art in its purest and most significant form can be best studied in the work of great modern artists like Paul Klee, Mondrian, Léger and Ben Nicholson. Klee, who died in 1939, probably did as much research into the resources of colour and shape and texture as any other artist in the twentieth century. He could put a few rectangles of subtly modulated colour on a small canvas or sheet of paper in such a way that they appeared to have more life and significance than many crowded figure compositions hung in the approved academies.

If you would like to carry out a simple experiment in the use of non-figurative shapes, you should consider one of the earliest designs made by Klee in the days when such departures from traditional practice were considered extremely daring. His picture contains one single flat shape—a light shape, on an

112

even dark background. Its silhouette is nothing like the silhouette of any known animal, bird, fish or insect, but it seems, when one has looked at it for a little while, as animal-like, bird-like, fish-like or insect-like as any illustration one could expect to see in the pages of a naturalists' handbook. It is no kind of beast, yet it could be any kind of beast. Can you design a shape that would be at once as non-committal and as capable of such varied interpretations as that? You may have to try several times before you find out how hard it is to do.

After that you can try to make a balanced and satisfying abstract design from a few simple geometric shapes (the artists who specialised in doing this called themselves 'suprematists'). Cut out from cardboard a square, an equilateral triangle, a circle and a hexagon and put them down in haphazard fashion on a piece of clean white paper so that each covers, or is partly covered by, part of one at least of the others. Then look carefully at the arrangement and ask yourself if it is a reasonably pleasant and interesting one to look at. If it is, draw round the outlines of the shapes with a sharp pencil, completing any part of an outline that has been hidden once the overlying shape has been taken away. If the arrangement does not satisfy you, move the cardboard pieces around until it does.

Then mix up some colours—a dark blue, for example, with two tints of blue: a very pale sky and a medium blue. Paint each of the shapes you have drawn on the paper with one of the colours, using the palest blue for the portions of your design that have been covered by one piece of cardboard only, the medium blue for the portions that have been covered by two pieces, and the dark blue for the portions that have been covered by three pieces. Then pick out the outer edge of the design with dark blue or black, as shown in Illustration 39. You would find it very instructive to complete and compare three or four of the many alternative arrangements that can be made from four flat geometric shapes in this way. Some arrangements will be much more satisfying aesthetically than others, and your task will be to separate the good from the disappointing. By exercising your discrimination and judgment over a simple problem like this you will learn some of the basic principles of two-dimensional design, and this knowledge will be useful if you decide to paint larger non-figurative pictures or abstract mural decorations.

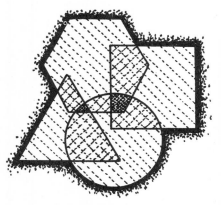

39. Geometric shapes can be combined to make interesting and decorative designs

After you have carried out a few experiments in purely geometric design, you may feel that you are not in sympathy with such mechanical shapes, and that you prefer figurative or representational work. Before you turn your back on abstract art for good, you should carry out a few designs in which natural forms are simplified or distorted slightly to suit the demands of a special set of conditions. For example, you can build up a 'motif' from shapes that suggest musical instruments or items of sporting equipment. Such semi-abstract designs can be seen, most proficiently carried out, in the pages of many of the best papers and magazines. The ability to derive pleasant and significant shapes from forms that do not need to be treated naturalistically is one of the most coveted skills a commercial artist can acquire.

SURREALISM) Most people wander in a strange half-world of fantasy and romance if they are allowed to lie in a drowsy state before they have to wake up properly in the morning. Certain twentieth-century painters—and a few earlier artists —have explored the pictorial possibilities of that half-world, or 'subconscious', and are known by critics who are anxious to classify their victims in neat categories as 'surrealists'.

The earlier artists referred to include Hieronymus Bosch, who peopled his haunted landscapes with wizards, devils, witches and other grotesque beings, Pieter Breughel the Elder, who would introduce a unique element of fantasy into his most carefully planned compositions, Henry Fuseli, who specialised in nightmares, John Martin, whose brother tried to burn down York Minster, and Richard Dadd, who conceived and executed some large and scrupulously detailed canvases while he was in detention in a lunatic asylum.

Among the best known of the twentith-century surrealists have been Salvador Dali, who, like Picasso, came originally from Spain, Yves Tanguy, who built up fantastic dream-land-scapes from meticulously painted abstract forms, and Max Ernst, whose 'pictures' were often constructed from wood, metal and other solid materials. Dali, whose technical virtuosity in paint has been one of the most remarkable phenomena of post-Cubist art, has always attracted a lot of attention—and publicity—by the strikingly erotic and morbid flavour of much of his work. In his paintings, forms that are normally stiffly mechanical, such as pocket watches, melt and drape themselves like warm wax over the edges of inadequate supporting sur-faces, shrubs and trees grow to resemble frighteningly authen-tic human faces, and male and female figures develop many

of the functional attributes of domestic furniture—his man
with a chest fitted with pull-out drawers being a notable
example. Yes, Dali's paintings can be as disquieting as the
writings of Freud and as full of fascinating detail as biological
specimens seen under the powerful lenses of an expensive
microscope.

You can get a lot of fun out of introducing a slight feeling
of inconsequence into your paintings, even if you do not feel
brave enough to try to reproduce your most disturbing dreams
in terms of paint. Look for a moment at the delightful titles
Paul Klee gave to some of his most charming pictures—
'Twittering Machine', 'Mount of the Sacred Cat' and 'She
Moos, We Play' are three examples—and you will see that
art that is faintly surrealist in flavour does not necessarily
have to be grim, alarming or macabre.

EXPRESSIONISM The tortured, emotionally supercharged
paintings of Vincent van Gogh were probably as largely re-
sponsible for the outbreak of expressionist painting in Germany in the early years of this century as any other stimulating
factors. Art teaching in Germany at that time tended to direct
all students into rigidly academic channels. The brilliant
colours, the frenzied textures and the supernaturally personal
vision of the psychopathic Dutchman sparked off an artistic
explosion the effects of which can still be felt today.

What is expressionist painting? That is one of the hardest
questions to answer that one could possibly be asked, since
thousands of paintings that could truly be called 'expressionist' have been produced without there being one single common
factor or characteristic in any ten of them. Perhaps it would
be easier to say what expressionist paintings are *not*: they are
not attempts to represent the outward appearance of any part
of the visible world, they are not exercises in beautiful or
lyrical composition, they are not in any sense of the words

116

poems in paint. If anything, they are attempts to explore the deepest, most mystical recesses of the soul, each artist's range of research being conditioned by his intensely individual circumstances of heredity and environment.

Expressionist pictures tend to be violent in colour, aggressive in their impact on the viewer's sensibilities and lacking in subservience to the traditional canons of composition and design. If you would like to paint expressionist pictures you will be—to use a colourful if somewhat hackneyed phrase— out on a limb. You will have to be your own teacher and your own guide. No one will be able to say that your pictures are good, or bad, by reference to any accepted standards, least of all the kind of standards you will find written about in a book. Until enough time has elapsed for the whole of twentieth-century painting to be seen in its proper perspective only one person will know if you have created genuine works of art or not. And you, yourself, will probably not be sure. But you will derive an enormous amount of excitement from the indecisiveness of it all, and the creativity.

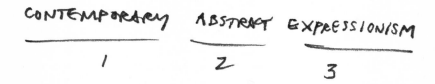

THIRTEEN

MOUNTING, FRAMING
AND HANGING YOUR WORK

Every artist finds at some time or another that he or she has
gone rather 'stale'—that ideas for new pictures will not come
easily, or that interest in a half-completed picture is difficult
to sustain. When this happens to you, turn your attention for
a while to the specialised problems of mounting, framing and
hanging some drawings or paintings you have already com-
pleted. Most unmounted and unframed pictures look slightly
unprepossessing to the inexperienced eye. You will almost
certainly find that the transformation you will see in your
pictures once they have been suitably presented will act like a
tonic, and you will be eager to pick up your pencil or brush
again as quickly as possible.

MOUNTING PICTURES   Pictures can be roughly divided into
two categories—those that look better on—or in—flat mounts,
and those that need thicker, heavier frames, as, for example,
frames made from wooden strips or mouldings. Among those
in the first category are pencil drawings, pen-and-ink sketches,
etchings, engravings, lithographs, architectural designs and
water colours; in the second category are all oil paintings
except the very slightest sketches. It is important to give each
of your works the appropriate type of setting—too heavy a
frame can overpower a tentative sketch that would be, if given
sufficient room to breathe, a very charming thing to look at.

To make a good job of mounting a picture, you may have
to do a certain amount of experimenting, as some works will
need wider margins than others. These trial layouts can be
most satisfactorily carried out with sheets of white cartridge

paper—some artists mount nearly all their sketches temporarily on paper, as soon as the sketches are finished. When you put a picture on a mount, see that the narrowest margin falls above the picture, and that the widest margin falls below it, as shown in Illustration 40. You can try another arrangement if you like, but the chances are that you will prefer the layout shown in the drawing. When you are satisfied, you can fix the picture temporarily to the mount by putting a small drop of paste

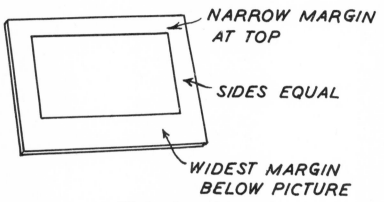

NARROW MARGIN AT TOP

SIDES EQUAL

WIDEST MARGIN BELOW PICTURE

40. This shows how a picture may be most pleasantly placed on a mount

or glue beneath each corner, but do not use much or you will not be able to detach the picture if you want to give it a more permanent mount or mat.

Mounting boards of various grades are stocked by most artists' materials suppliers, and among the kinds you will be offered will be some that have delicately tinted, toned and textured surfaces. The choice of a suitable mat for any particular picture is entirely a matter of taste and sound judgment, and those can only be developed by a long process of trial and error. At first, you may be tempted by boards that sound really appealing, such as those surfaced in 'warm stone' or 'old rose', or by boards with a finish that closely imitates suède, but if you are wise you will use any boards but matt white, ivory or cream with the greatest hesitation. A little extra richness and distinction can be added to plain mounts by the use of some straight lines, drawn parallel to the sides of the picture with a sharp pencil and ruler, or with a straight edge and ruling pen. If the space between one of these pairs of lines is tinted with a colour chosen from one of the colours that predominate in the picture, the mount will have a specially luxurious quality that will amply repay you for the extra trouble you have taken.

If you are making a mount from a fairly thick board of good quality, you can cut a bevelled mat, fixing your picture behind this instead of sticking it on the front surface. To cut a set of bevels you will need a very sharp knife or a new steel-backed razor blade and a metal ruler or straight edge (if you use a piece of wood to guide the cutter you will probably slice some shavings off it).

First, find the position on the mat that suits the picture best, and mark the positions of the corners with faint pencil crosses. Then take the picture away and draw the boundary lines of the bevels. These will not run exactly from cross to cross, but a little way inside them, so that the mat will eventually hide the edges of the picture and cover a strip about $\frac{1}{16}$ in. wide all round its perimeter.

Then press your straight edge down along any one of the boundary lines with your left hand (if you are right handed) and with your free hand slide your cutting edge along it at an angle of 45°, as shown in Illustration 41. If possible, the blade should pass right through the board at the first cut. A second cut, if it is called for, may bring a sliver of board away like a length of bacon rind. The other three sides should be bevelled in exactly the same way, then the picture can be fixed in position with small pieces of gummed tape. When you can cut bevels quickly and decisively you will be able to give all your sketches that are worth special treatment an extra-attractive mat.

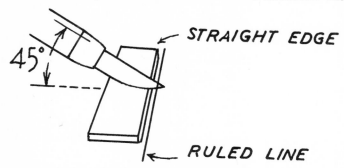

STRAIGHT EDGE

45°

RULED LINE

41. Cutting a bevelled mat is fairly simple if you have a sharp knife and a metal straight edge

PASSE PARTOUT You can protect your mounted pictures from dirt and other harmful factors by keeping them in boxes or portfolios, by covering them with cellophane, or by glazing them. Passe partout provides one of the easiest ways of giving a picture a more or less permanent glazed frame. You will need, for each picture that you wish to protect and display in this way:

A *sheet of glass*, that is exactly the same size as the mount. A more or less rigid *backing board* that is also the same size as the mount. Thick cardboard, hardboard or even plywood can be used for this—strawboard is rather pulpy, and may swell and warp as it grows older.

One or two *hangers*. These can be lengths of tape, the ends of which are pushed through slots in the background and then glued to its inside surface. Alternatively, you can buy special hangers, each of which consists of a metal ring with two tongues. The tongues are pushed through a slot in the backboard, flattened, and then covered with a piece of gummed tape.

121

Passe partout. Special gummed strips for passe partout are marketed in a good range of colours and textures, and can be bought at most stationers' shops. The choice of a strip may well be affected by the predominating colours in a picture—for example, a hot sunlit landscape pitched mainly in yellows, oranges and browns may look splendid in a cream mount edged with gold. A silver border could conceivably 'kill' the whole scheme.

When you have assembled your materials, cut off four strips of binding from your selected roll. Each strip should be about half an inch longer than the side it is to bind. Then put the glass, mount and backing board together, keeping them in their correct relative positions with Bulldog clips or sprung clothes pegs. Most passe partout bindings sold nowadays are lightly scored at the factory, so you will find it quite easy to wrap each of the strips you have cut off over the edge you intend it to bind. Do this carefully before you apply any water to the adhesive or you will find that the strip is too sticky to handle.

Then moisten the back of each strip thoroughly, using a small pad of cotton wool or piece of sponge that you have soaked in water. Make sure that every part of the adhesive has been damped, or the strip may peel off the glass in time. When the strip is ready, leave it damp side up on your working surface, and take up the assembled picture. Lay the edge to be bound along the strip between the previously made creases, and fold the sides of the strip over on to the front and back of the picture. Then repeat the process on the opposite side of the picture, leaving the sides that lie between until you have trimmed the first mitres (a 'mitre' in this context is a line cut at 45° ending at the corner of the picture).

To trim the mitres, you will need a 45° set square—you cannot hope to guess the angles correctly with any certainty of success—and a very sharp knife or steel-backed razor blade. Pull the waste ends of strip away very carefully. If you disturb any part that is to remain on the glass or backing board re-moisten the adhesive and apply a little pressure with your finger nail. When the mitres are complete, apply the strips of binding to the intermediate sides, trim their ends, and then leave the frame to dry for at least a day before you attempt to clean the glass.

If you fancy a bi-coloured passe partout edging for one of your pictures, you can use two harmonious or contrasted bindings, applying one to the other in such a way that a thin band of the lower binding is left uncovered by the upper bind-ing. Illustration 42 should make this clear.

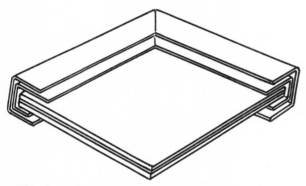

42. This shows how bi-coloured passe partout edgings are made. Only one corner of the picture is shown in the drawing, of course

SOLID FRAMES For oil paintings and any other pictures that may need heavier frames than passe partout will provide you can use ready made frames if you can afford them, carved frames if money is no problem at all, and frames built from the excellent mouldings sold by nearly all timber merchants if you have to economise.

123

To mitre the ends of the four sides of a frame accurately—
if you decide to fabricate one for yourself—you will need a
mitre block like the one shown on the left of Illustration 43,
or a slightly larger and heavier mitre box. These are, of course,
for keeping the blade of a saw exactly upright and at the correct
angle while a cut is being made.

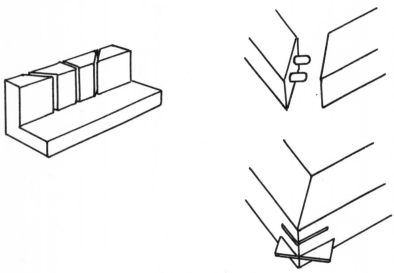

43. A mitre block (left)
and two easy methods of strengthening a corner joint (right)

To join the mitred ends of two pieces of moulding, you can
use one of the modern cements or contact glues that do not
need to be heated. If one of these is used alone, the frame may
not be strong enough to stand a lot of wear and tear, but it is
easy to reinforce the joints; two methods are shown on the
right of Illustration 43. In the upper drawing, two small
pegs made from wooden dowel rod are inserted in holes drilled
into the two pieces of moulding. These holes should be a fairly

easy push fit for the pegs so that a little glue can be applied to all surfaces before the final assembly is made. In the lower drawing you can see how saw cuts can be carefully made across a mitred end so that pieces of veneer can be inserted— also with the addition of a little glue. When this glue has had plenty of time to harden, the pieces of veneer can be trimmed with a sharp knife so that they are exactly flush with the frame.

Unpainted, unvarnished wooden frames can be quite attractive, but you will probably want to apply paint or some other covering material to most of the frames you make yourself. You can use ordinary household paints, either brushed on in flat coats or stippled on with crumpled newspapers; you can use polish, if the mouldings are made from any particularly fine timber; you can use a mixture of size and slaked plaster or size and whiting; you can try gilding or burnishing the mouldings; or you can cover them with cloth of any suitable kind. Look at the frames in any well-presented exhibition of paintings and you will come home with plenty of ideas.

HANGING PICTURES   However good a picture may be, it can always be spoiled by being hung incorrectly. It is especially important to use a certain amount of discrimination in an ordinary living room, where light entering the room from awkwardly situated windows can cause an annoying amount of glare and shine. As a general rule, a wall in which there is a large window will be a particularly unsuitable place for hanging pictures, and a wall that is directly opposite a large window may not be much more satisfactory. If you have any choice in the matter, use walls that are at right angles to the direction in which the light is falling, but do not decide the position of any picture too finally until you have made a few tentative experiments. These notes may help you:

Don't place your pictures too high on any wall, or you will

not be able to look at them without a certain amount of strain, and that is fatal to all visual enjoyment.

Don't place pictures of differing sizes at different levels, or the effect they produce may be just as disturbing. If you hang all the pictures in a room in such a way that all their *lower* edges are exactly the same height from the floor, the general impression they give will be one of well-ordered simplicity.

Don't let a picture hang askew. If you insert near the top of each frame two of the closed rings sold specially for the purpose, you can make a running loop quite easily from a single length of picture cord, as shown in Illustration 44. The level of a picture hung in this way can be altered at a moment's notice, literally with one touch of a finger.

Don't let a picture hang too long without asking yourself if anyone is still getting some stimulus from it. It is all too easy to let a picture become part of the accustomed and monotonous background to general living. Once one of your paintings ceases to interest you, take it away and paint another to replace it. A true artist is always looking to the future, rather than the past.

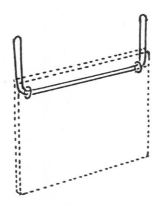

44. A running loop is used for picture hanging

INDEX

127